The Rights of All Our Children

A Plea for Action

Evans Clinchy

HEINEMANN
Portsmouth, NH

Heinemann
A division of Reed Elsevier Inc.
361 Hanover Street
Portsmouth, NH 03801–3912
www.heinemann.com

Offices and agents throughout the world

The author and publisher wish to thank those who have generously given permission to reprint borrowed material:

Excerpts from *The Making of Intelligence: Evolution, Development, and Psychology* by Ken Richardson. Copyright © 1998. Published by Weidenfeld & Nicolson, London. Reprinted by permission of the publisher.

Library of Congress Cataloging-in-Publication Data
Clinchy, Evans.
    The rights of all our children : a plea for action / Evans Clinchy.
      p.   cm.
Includes bibliographical references and index.
    ISBN 0-325-00396-3 (alk. paper)
   1. Educational equalization—United States.   2. Minorities—
Education—United States.   3. Privatization in education—United States.
4. Education—Standards—United States.   I. Title.

LC213.2 .C55   2002
379.2'6—dc21   2002004504

Editor: Lois Bridges
Production editor: Sonja S. Chapman
Cover design: Jenny Jensen Greenleaf
Compositor: TechBooks
Manufacturing: Steve Bernier

Printed in the United States of America on acid-free paper
06 05 04 03 02 DA 1 2 3 4 5

For
SeanRoss

Contents

Acknowledgments

This book began life as an article in the educational journal *Phi Delta Kappan,* and therefore my first thanks must go to the editors of that journal, Pauline B. Gough, Bruce M. Smith, and Rise Koben, for their unflagging support of my work. That article was then picked up by my superb editor at Heinemann, Lois Bridges, who with untiring enthusiasm asked that it be turned into a book.

I'd also like to mention a partial list of mentors, models, colleagues, and just plain friends, past and present, without whose example, encouragement, and in many cases active assistance this book would not have been possible. These include (but are hardly limited to) Harold Howe II; Seymour Bernard Sarason; Deborah Meier; Sy Fliegel; Alfie Kohn; Susan Ohanian; Monty Neill and Karen Hartke, of FairTest; Patrick Mogan and George Tspatsaris, of the Lowell, Massachusetts, Public Schools; Roland Charpentier, of the Worcester, Massachusetts, Public Schools; William H. Ohrenberger, Edward Doherty, Larry Myatt, and Linda Nathan, of the Boston, Massachusetts, Public Schools; Robert Fried and James Fraser, of Northeastern University; and Karen Mapp, Owen Heleen, and Don Davies, of the Institute for Responsive Education.

And finally, of course, thanks to my beloved wife, Blythe McVicker Clinchy, who makes everything possible.

1

The Slow Death of Our Educational Civil Rights

N ow that the great American post–World War II civil rights movement in education has run its course and in fact is moving rapidly backward, it is time to launch a new educational civil rights movement—or at least take the old one in a new and more comprehensive direction appropriate for the twenty-first century.

I think most people would agree that the Supreme Court's 1954 *Brown v Board of Education* decision[1] was the twentieth century's great recognition that all the children and all the parents in this country have federal educational rights guaranteed by the U.S. Constitution. That *Brown* decision made three vitally important rulings that have—or should have—forever changed the American system of public education.

The first was to overturn the long legal tradition in this country stating that since the Constitution makes no specific reference to education, the control of the nation's public schools must be left solely in the hands of state governments. The Court found that in cases in which the Fourteenth Amendment (which guarantees "the equal protection of the laws") or any other part of the Bill of Rights has been violated, the federal courts could exercise jurisdiction and order a remedy.

This led to a second great ruling that the "segregation of children in public schools solely on the basis of race deprives children of the minority group of equal educational opportunities, even though the physical facilities and other 'tangible' factors may be equal."

A third and perhaps even more revolutionary finding was: "In these days, it is doubtful that any child may reasonably be expected to succeed in life if he [or she] is denied the opportunity of an education. *Such an opportunity, where*

1

a state has undertaken to provide an opportunity for an education in its public schools, is a right which must be made available to all on equal terms" (emphasis added).

Following *Brown* and other subsequent court decisions, this country embarked on a decades-long effort not only to desegregate all of our public schools but to provide *all* American children of every color and ethnic group with those "equal educational opportunities."

Not Wholly a Success

If we look at what has happened since 1954, however, we see all too clearly that that movement has turned out to be only a qualified success. Yes, legal segregation has been ended in this country, and southern school districts can no longer run forcibly segregated schools. But many school districts—especially inner-city districts in both the North and the South—are at least as segregated as they were in 1954. Those in major cities like New York, Los Angeles, Boston, and Chicago are even *more* segregated. According to studies conducted by the Civil Rights Project at Harvard University, what we now have is "accelerating resegregation of the South and the continuation of a long and relentless march toward even more severe segregation for Latino students as they become our largest minority."[2]

Further, both federal and state courts are now declaring that many formerly segregated districts have made "good faith"—even if unsuccessful—efforts to desegregate and are therefore legally "unified" and relieved of any further duty to integrate their schools. These same courts are also declaring that "race-based" admissions policies are unconstitutional and that districts may now return to the policy of racially identifiable "neighborhood" schools, the very policy that caused northern de facto segregation in the first place. The Harvard study authors concluded, "We are floating back toward an educational pattern that has never in the nation's history produced equal and successful schools. . . . Reversing the trends of intensifying segregation and inequality will be difficult, but the costs of passively accepting them are likely to be immense."[3]

In addition to these retreats on racial and ethnic desegregation, we now have increasing *economic* segregation throughout our system of public education as well. That same Harvard study found:

> Though we usually think of segregation in racial and ethnic terms, it's important to also realize that the spreading segregation has a strong class component. When African-American and Latino students are segregated in schools where the majority of students are nonwhite, they are very likely to

find themselves in schools where poverty is concentrated. This is, of course, not the case with segregated white students, whose majority white schools almost always enroll high proportions of students from the middle class. This is a crucial difference, because concentrated poverty is linked to lower educational achievement.

School-level poverty is related to many variables that affect a school's overall chance at successfully educating students, including parental education levels, availability of advanced courses, teachers with credentials in the subject they are teaching, instability of enrollment, dropouts, untreated health problems, lower college-going rates and many other important factors.[4]

Ignoring the Realities of Poverty and Class

This continuing concentration of both poor and minority students in our struggling, underfunded urban school systems was cemented in place by the Supreme Court's ruling in the 1974 *Milliken v Bradley* case involving the desegregation of the Detroit, Michigan, schools. The lower courts in that case had ruled in favor of a metropolitan desegregation plan requiring the participation of the city's predominantly wealthy and white suburban school districts. The Supreme Court, however, ruled against not only the Detroit plan but all compulsory metropolitan desegregation plans unless the suburban districts could be proved to have behaved with deliberate segregative intent, a case almost impossible to make. Segregated white suburban districts throughout the country thus could not be forced to join with minority segregated urban districts to both desegregate and improve the education offered minority children in those urban districts.[5]

In 1973 that same Supreme Court produced a decision that essentially negated the Brown "equal terms" decision and relieved the states of any federal constitutional necessity to make sure that the education of all children in every state is fully and equally funded. The *San Antonio v Rodriguez* decision essentially banned any reading of *Brown* arguing that education is a federal constitutional right under the Fourteenth Amendment and the phrase "equal terms" therefore requires the federal government to guarantee equal funding of the education of all children. The Court thus decided that it is constitutionally permissible for enormous disparities in funding to continue to exist between rich and poor school districts throughout the country.[6]

So inner-city schools still not only house most of our minority children and young people but most of our poor children as well—that is, all those children with the social and educational handicaps listed in the Harvard study. And all too many of these inner-city schools are still very clearly victims of Jonathan Kozol's "savage inequalities." While suburban school districts may spend as much fifteen thousand dollars on every student, city and rural school districts are fortunate if they can raise seven or eight thousand. Those urban students and their teachers are living what Kozol and Minnesota's Senator Paul Wellstone have described as "a familiar story." Our inner-city school systems, they say, are still "burdened by impoverished students, insufficient funding and decrepit buildings. . . . And politicians and business leaders condemn the schools as dysfunctional."[7] It is all too true that inner-city students often are not only housed in ancient, crumbling buildings but also taught in classes of thirty-five to forty-five students staffed by undertrained and underpaid teachers. They often are poorly supplied with ancient educational materials and little or no modern electronic equipment. And all too often they have totally inadequate support services outside school.

As if all these social malfeasances were not enough, we must face the appalling fact that they are happening at a time when we are not only the richest nation the world has ever seen but a nation in which the already rich are garnering an ever increasing share of the national wealth. According to a Congressional Budget Office report issued in 2001, during the period from 1979 to 1997 the average after-tax income of the wealthiest one percent of the American population rose by 157 percent (from $263,700 to $677,900) while the lowest-earning 20 percent saw their after-tax income drop from $10,900 to $10,800.[8] Meanwhile, twenty million children and their families are still living in poverty. Neither those children nor their parents even have adequate health insurance, to say nothing of adequate schools, adequate social services, or adequate jobs.

Still Not the Full Disaster

But that is not all. We now have four movements abroad in the land that are directly aimed at destroying the great American democratic tradition of the local control of public education through locally elected boards of education and local school districts. These movements are thus attempting to remove educational control from the parents and other local citizens who are directly affected by the schools and who are still primarily responsible for supporting them.

Charter Schools

This movement began with great hopes some twenty years ago. Along with many other people, charter advocates were genuinely disturbed by what they saw as the low quality of many—particularly urban—schools and the almost total lack of choice within the typical public school system.

These advocates were also concerned about the lack of innovation in public schools—the inability of local districts to create and test new ideas that might dramatically improve American public education. They attributed these failures in no small measure to the bureaucratic rules and regulations and the restrictive union contracts that prevented individual schools from exercising the philosophical, curricular, staffing, and financial autonomy necessary for both high-quality schooling and innovation.

The solution they came up with was that state governments should authorize and fund (i.e., *charter*) the creation of public schools that are relatively independent of any local district, schools that could then be free of the bureaucratic rules, regulations, and union contracts. In most cases these have been new small schools that parents can choose as alternatives to their local district schools.

It was hoped that charter schools would be a source of free market competition for local districts, provide successful and most likely innovative models that could be adopted by the districts, and offer parents locked into demonstrably failing schools a viable escape route.

Over the past two decades, the charter movement has succeeded in enabling just about every state in the nation to create a system of such relatively independent schools. While in most cases charters draw their funding from the local district in which they have been created and must have a racial and ethnic student population similar to that of their district, they are independent in terms of curriculum, staffing, and expenditures. Again in almost all cases, however, charters must meet the state's academic standards, must administer the state "high stakes" tests, and are supervised by state education authorities to ensure—at least in theory—adequate legal and financial performance.

In support of the charter idea, the competition charter schools provide has prompted some local school districts to create what are essentially in-district charters—that is, district schools that have the same kinds of autonomy granted to charters but that are supervised by their locally elected school board. Boston is a good example, having created ten "pilot" schools that both parents and staff members (teachers/principals) can choose to become part of. New York City now has more than a hundred new small "alternative" schools that are attempting—many of them quite successfully—to operate on charterlike principles. "Pilot" or "alternative" schools can be a major part of the new educational reform and civil rights movement we are espousing, but only if they are not destroyed by the standards-and-testing agenda that threatens to erase their autonomy and turn them into clones of traditional schools.

Vouchers

The second movement aimed at destroying our local school districts is the movement to turn large segments of the public educational enterprise over to private and parochial schools by offering publicly funded vouchers to help parents pay private and parochial school tuition.

As with charter schools, the original voucher proponents were concerned not only about the reputed low quality and rigid bureaucracy of the public schools but most especially about the lack of parental choice. They therefore proposed that all parents be given a voucher for each child roughly equal to the local district's cost per pupil or the average state funding per pupil. Parents would be free to choose a public, private, or parochial school and, in the case of the private or parochial school, apply the voucher toward the cost of tuition.

This movement is bogged down in legal problems over the use of public money to fund private schools and, in the case of parochial schools, the separation of church and state set up by the First Amendment. So far, there are only two quite limited operating examples of voucher programs, one in Milwaukee and one in Cleveland. More on this a bit later.

Privatization

A third movement endangering our local districts is the move to turn large segments of public education over to the profit-making private sector by hiring corporations to run individual schools or even whole school systems. This movement and its problems are discussed in greater detail in Chapter 4.

Standards and Testing

The fourth and perhaps most dangerous movement is the new national educational agenda of imposing uniform, standardized "higher" academic standards and uniform, standardized "high stakes" testing on all schools, all parents, and all students. These standards and tests are not developed and implemented at the local level but are, without the direct consent of those being governed or tested, devised and then mandated by state legislative and educational authorities who may or may not be aware of the vast differences that exist among any state's local communities and the individual students within those communities. This authoritarian, one-size-fits-all standards-and-testing agenda has now been adopted by the Bush administration and the U.S. Congress as the official national education policy, requiring the testing of all students in all grades from three through eight and punishing both students and their schools if the students fail the tests.

As we shall see later, there are many arguments that can be and are being raised against authoritarian, antidemocratic, one-size-fits-all standards and testing. But one immediate question any such agenda raises is whether parents have a right to refuse to have their children subjected to the agenda and its tests, if they believe the tests to be harmful and thus not in the best educational interests of their children.

The answer to this question is murky at best and is still very much in the process of resolution—or irresolution—all across the country. At the moment, according to an informal, not-yet-completed study being conducted by the Minnesota Department of Children, Families, and Learning, at least six states—Minnesota, New Mexico, Rhode Island, Georgia, California, and Kentucky—allow parents to opt out. In Minnesota and Georgia, however, this means that a student cannot receive a high school diploma, while in Rhode Island parents are warned that such action will adversely affect their children's schools. Five other states—South Carolina, Alabama, Connecticut, Illinois, and Massachusetts—do not allow opting out, but many parents are simply boycotting the tests, and organized parent, teacher, and civil rights groups are mounting legislative and legal protests against such abrogation of parent rights.

Nor do most states make any provision for the right of local school boards, teachers, and school administrators to refuse to give the tests if they believe them to be harmful and not in the best interests of their students. Much more on all this a bit later.

Moving Rapidly Backward

What all these legal and social retreats and movements add up to is a concerted—even if in many cases possibly unwitting—campaign not only to undermine the democratic structure of American public education but also to alter radically the traditional democratic aims and purposes of that system. We as a nation are not only failing to fulfill the right of all American children to have a fair, just, and equal public education, we are also making the American system of public education, which has never been as fair, just, and equal as it should or could have been, even less fair, less just, and less equal than it was during the twenty or so years immediately following the *Brown* decision.

Not Just *Brown*

In addition to the rights guaranteed by the U.S. Constitution and upheld by *Brown*, a further set of educational rights is set forth in another landmark twentieth-century document—the Universal Declaration of Human Rights developed by the United Nations immediately after World War II and ratified by the United States in December of 1948.[9] After setting forth the basic requirements for a truly democratic society in its first twenty-four articles, the Declaration has some pertinent things to say about what responsibilities all democratic governments have not just to children in the public schools but to the families and the local communities from which those children come.

The first part of Article 25 of the Declaration, for instance, says that "everyone has the right to a standard of living adequate for the health and well-being of himself and his family [and I assume herself and her family], including food, clothing, housing and medical care and necessary social services and the right to security in the event of unemployment, sickness, disability, widowhood, old age or other lack of livelihood in circumstances beyond his [or her] control." And the second part of that article says, "Motherhood and childhood are entitled to special care and assistance. All children, whether born in or out of wedlock, shall enjoy the same social protection."

Article 26 of the Declaration, speaking directly to the educational rights of all parents, all children, and all young people, says first, "Everyone has a right to education. Education shall be free [i.e., publicly supported] at least at the elementary and fundamental stages. Technical and professional education shall be made generally available and higher education shall be equally accessible to all on the basis of merit." The article then goes on to state the two fundamental rights that are most directly relevant here: "Education shall be directed to the full development of the human personality and to the strengthening of respect for human rights and fundamental freedoms," and "Parents have a prior right to choose the kind of education that shall be given to their children."

A Catalog of Fundamental Educational Rights and Their Current Violations

In these two great statements, *Brown* and the Universal Declaration outlining the social and educational rights of all children and parents in any truly democratic society, we have the foundation for a new civil rights movement. If we could implement a system of public education based on these rights, we would at last bring about that fair, just, and equal system of public schooling we have been attempting to build in this country for the past three hundred years.

Those rights—and the flagrant violations of those rights currently taking place in the United States—can be summed up in this fashion:

- The right of all parents and children to equal access to all educational opportunities as guaranteed by the first part of the *Brown* decision—that is, no legal or (most important now) no de facto segregated schools. The flagrant violation here is the continued existence, almost fifty years after *Brown,* of those urban schools with student and parent bodies made up heavily (or entirely) of the poor and minority segments of the population.

- The right of all parents and children to equal funding of the schools attended by those children. The continuing and flagrant violation here is of the *Brown* decision's equal-terms finding and thus the continuing tolerance of gross disparities in funding between rich, primarily suburban districts and those inner-city and rural districts that are composed mainly of poor and minority children.

- The right of all parents and children to full and equal opportunities to learn. The flagrant violation here is the continuing gross disparity between the learning opportunities offered to students in our richly endowed suburban schools and those provided students in our decaying and underfunded urban schools.

- The right of parents and other local citizens to control the content and procedures of the public education offered to the children in their local public schools. The flagrant violation here is the powerful movement on the part of both federal and state governments, through standards-and-testing mandates, increasingly to impose nonlocally determined orthodoxies of intellectual content and educational pedagogy on all parents and students in public schools all across the land. This includes the violation of the First Amendment free speech/academic freedom rights of local teachers, principals, and system administrators, working as equal partners with parents, to make and implement professional decisions about the conduct of local public schooling. Although there is as yet no body of federal case law supporting these rights for K–12 teachers and principals, arguments for them can and should be made by the two national teachers unions, all other K–12 professional organizations, and the American Civil Liberties Union, using the First Amendment academic freedom rights established for faculty members in our colleges and universities as precedent.

- The right of all children and young people to the full development of their human personalities—that is, the full development of *all* their innate intellectual, artistic, social, and moral capacities. The first flagrant violation here is the imposition of narrow curricular and therefore narrow intellectual orthodoxies on all students through the mandating of uniform, strictly academic standards and uniform, standardized high-stakes testing. But a second violation is the imposition in the case of poor and minority students of compulsory remedial tracks and specialized remedial programs that foreclose curricular opportunities and thus narrow their learning to only the most basic skills and uninspired and uninspiring knowledge.

- The right of parents to choose the *kind* of public schooling their children will receive and the concurrent right of teachers and other educational professionals in the public schools to practice the kind of schooling they believe is best for the children and young people placed in their care. The first flagrant violation here is the rigid, antidemocratic, and heavily bureaucratic organization of virtually all of our existing local school systems, an organization that denies both parents and professional staff the ability first to identify and then to choose the kind of education they believe is best. A second and equally important violation is the standards-and-testing movement that is further forcing all schools to become standardized clones of one another. This violation includes ignoring the previously stated right of parents not to have their children subjected to federal, state, or local standardized testing, a right that minimally requires prohibiting schools and school systems from conducting such tests unless and until they have the *written* consent of parents.

These rights are the core of the needed new civil rights movement, a movement that must remedy all of the violations described above.

2

The Record So Far: Desegregation and Fiscal Equity

I f we accept the two parts of the *Brown* decision guaranteeing all students a desegregated education on equal terms, we are first faced with the fundamental fact that the education of every American child must, in so far as this is humanly possible, take place in racially, ethnically, and economically integrated schools that receive equal financial support.

Desegregation

The history of the past fifty years tells us that providing minority children in this country with schools and school systems that are truly and equally integrated is difficult and perhaps impossible. That same history has also shown us that some of the more outrageously coercive ways in which we have approached that task have turned out to be not only socially disastrous but also educationally unproductive for the very children they were designed to help. But whatever that history has been and whatever the odds against success may be, those fifty years have told us as well that all is not lost, that there still may be successful approaches to both social and educational integration.

As briefly mentioned in the previous chapter, the Supreme Court's five-to-four 1974 *Milliken v Bradley* decision involving the desegregation of the Detroit, Michigan, schools held that suburban districts could not be part of a desegregation solution unless they were themselves found guilty of deliberately segregative practices, a condition that it is virtually impossible to prove legally. This decision goes a long way toward explaining the Harvard Project findings attesting to "accelerating resegregation of the South and the continuation of a long and relentless march toward even more severe segregation" in the North.

11

The District Court and the Appeals Court in the *Milliken* case found both Detroit and the state of Michigan guilty of de jure segregation but made no attempt to find the suburban districts specifically guilty. However, in fashioning a remedy, both courts found that a Detroit-only solution would still leave all Detroit schools predominantly and identifiably black, since the system was 64 percent black. Both courts therefore decided that an interdistrict solution was required involving the nearby (and virtually all-white) suburban systems. Both the plaintiffs and defendants agreed that such a metropolitan plan would not only produce genuine desegregation but also require much less forced busing than a Detroit-only plan would.

The Supreme Court, however, by their five-to-four vote, dismissed both lower court findings and instructed the plaintiffs to go back and forge a Detroit-only desegregation plan, the plan that is currently in place in that city. This barring of suburban participation in big-city integration planning is currently the law of the land.

This decision led to one of the many eloquent dissents filed by Justice Thurgood Marshall:

> In *Brown v Board of Education,* this Court held that segregation of children in public schools on the basis of race deprives minority group children of equal educational opportunities and therefore denies them the equal protection of the laws under the Fourteenth Amendment. This Court recognized that remedying decades of segregation in public education would not be an easy task. Subsequent events, unfortunately, have seen that prediction bear bitter fruit. . . . After twenty years of small, often difficult steps toward that great end, the Court today takes a giant step backwards. . . .
>
> I cannot subscribe to this emasculation of our constitutional guarantee of equal protection of the laws, and I must respectfully dissent. Our precedents, in my view, firmly establish that where, as here, state-imposed segregation has been demonstrated, it becomes the duty of the state to eliminate root and branch all vestiges of racial discrimination and to achieve the greatest possible degree of actual desegregation. . . .
>
> The rights at issue in this case are too fundamental to be abridged on the grounds as superficial as those relied on by the majority today. We deal here with the right of all our children, whatever their race, to an equal start in life and to equal opportunity to reach their full potential as citizens. Those children who have been denied that right in the past deserve better than to see fences thrown up to deny them that right in the future. Our nation, I fear, will be ill served by the Court's refusal to remedy separate and unequal education, for unless our children begin to learn together, there is little hope that our people will ever learn to live together.[10]

Fiscal Equality

The 1973 *Rodriguez* suit arguing for fiscal equality was brought by minority plaintiffs in Edgewood, Texas, the poorest school district in the state, located in the core-city sector of San Antonio. These parents argued that their students (96 percent poor Mexican Americans and African Americans) were supported during the 1967–68 school year by only $356 per pupil while the students in nearby Alamo Heights, the most affluent school district in the city, received $594 per pupil. This discrepancy was due, they argued, to the greater ability of the wealthy residents of Alamo Heights to raise local school funding over and above the contributions of the state and federal governments.

The federal district court ruled for the plaintiffs. That lower court, first, upheld the *Brown* decision that education is "a fundamental right" of the citizens of this country. The court then further concluded that the discrepancy in funding did indeed violate the U.S. Constitution's Fourteenth Amendment guaranteeing the equal protection of the laws. The Supreme Court, by another narrow five-to-four decision, reversed both of these findings and thus validated and continued the situation we have today whereby poor and minority parents throughout the country must rely on state-by-state constitutionality cases even to begin to obtain equal funding for their children.

In the *Rodriguez* case, Justice Marshall issued another of his eloquent dissents, remarking that:

> The Court today decides, in effect, that a state may constitutionally vary the quality of education which it offers its children in accordance with the amount of taxable wealth located in the school districts within which they reside. The majority's decision represents an abrupt departure from the mainstream of recent state and federal court decisions concerning the unconstitutionality of state educational financing depending on taxable local wealth. . . .
>
> More unfortunately, though, the majority's holding can only be seen as a retreat from our historic commitment to equality of educational opportunity and as unsupportable acquiescence in a system which deprives children in their earliest years of the chance to reach their full potential as citizens. The Court does this despite the absence of any substantial justification for a scheme which arbitrarily channels educational resources in accordance with the fortuity of the amount of taxable wealth within each district.[11]

Some Flickers of Hope?

It is true that many states, forced by lawsuits brought under their state constitutions, are attempting to equalize state funding of their local school districts. But while some of these states, such as Hawaii, Texas, and Vermont, have managed to create a more equal distribution of state money, even they have as yet not been able to eliminate the spending disparities between rich districts and poor districts completely. In most cases, any such "equality" is not being achieved by using new state funding to bring the $7,000 or $8,000 in the poor districts up to the $12,00 or $15,000 of the rich districts. Rather, small amounts of additional state money are added to the budgets of the poor districts but only to the always limited extent that state politics will allow.

In at least one case—Vermont—state funding allotted to rich districts is transferred to poorer districts. According to a report entitled *Educational Equity in Vermont*, before the remedial legislation went into effect in 1998 the wealthier towns in the state spent on average $2,000 more per student than the poorer districts did. By 2001, the state distributed a roughly uniform $5,200 per student to every local district and the per-pupil difference between wealthier and poorer districts had dropped to $500. Supporters of the legislation hope that, politics permitting, the gap will be closed by the end of the three-year phasing-in process.[12]

"Politics permitting" means, of course, that there has been enormous political resistance on the part of people in the rich districts who do not wish to give up their well-funded schools. Some of these districts have set up private charitable tax-exempt foundations to which citizens may voluntarily contribute in order to maintain their previous funding levels without raising taxes. Supporters of the equalization legislation, however, are taking legal action against these foundations, arguing that it was never the purpose of such foundations to use tax-exempt money to pay for services that normally are and should be tax supported.

While this attitude on the part of parents in richer and therefore relatively well-funded districts may at first glance appear ungenerous, the fairest solution to this problem is clearly not simply to Robin-Hood money from the rich districts and give it to the poor ones but rather to raise the funding of the poor districts up to the level of the rich ones.

In some cases, despite attempts to equalize funding, the situation is getting worse. In Milwaukee, Wisconsin, for instance, the state's funding formula was declared unconstitutional in 1976 and a new funding formula was later instituted. According to a new report issued this year by the nonprofit research group Rethinking Schools, in 1980 the white and African American populations in the Milwaukee Public Schools were roughly equal. At that time, per-pupil spending in Milwaukee was $265 above the state average and only $127 below the suburban average. By 1988, however, the Milwaukee schools comprised 80 percent students of color and per-pupil spending was $506 below the state average and $1,254 below the suburban average.[13]

It is also possible that a suit currently under way in federal court in California may make a contribution here. In that case, the American Civil Liberties Union is suing the state in what it hopes will be a class action suit on behalf of all poor, minority, and special needs children in the state's underfunded schools in an attempt to force the state to bring the curricular and facilities standards up to those in the better-funded districts.[14]

While the *Rodriguez* decision supports the existing inequitable system of school financing by saying that this is a matter for states to decide, the Supreme Court in that decision did hold out a flicker of hope. The final paragraph of the decision says, "We hardly need add that this Court's action is not to be viewed as placing its judicial imprimatur on the status quo. The need is apparent for reform in tax systems which may well have relied too long and too heavily on the local property tax. And certainly innovative thinking as to public education, its methods, and its funding is necessary to insure both a higher level of quality and greater uniformity of opportunity."[15]

This language and the Vermont example raise the possibility that the answer to the problem of unequal funding may eventually be that states should implement a progressive state property tax solely for educational purposes, with the revenue being redistributed to local school districts on a statewide per-pupil basis but with special weight given to districts serving poor, minority, and special needs children. This would be similar to the progressive income tax, whereby wealthy citizens pay more than poor citizens but those poor citizens may, because of greater need, receive a proportionately greater share of the governmental expenditures.

3

Subverting Public Education: Charters and Vouchers

If the fight for constitutionally guaranteed desegregation and equal funding for all children is at the moment still very much in the balance, the assault on the democratic structure of American public education—that is, the tradition of local citizen control through locally elected boards of education—continues apace.

We need to be clear here. While basic equity issues like desegregation, equal funding, and an organizational structure based on local control are all fundamental to any democratic system of public schooling, this does not mean that they will automatically produce the fair, just, and equal educational system this country should have. To achieve a truly equitable system, we must also address and solve the questions of educational quality and all children's access to that quality.

I do not, of course, mean "quality" as defined by the new high-standards-high-stakes-testing agenda, in which an authoritarian, antidemocratic, one-size-fits-all form of education is imposed on all students, all parents, all teachers, and all schools in every state. Quite the opposite. While the advocates of that agenda speak nobly about how "all children can learn" and about "leaving no child behind," the measures they are advocating will in reality guarantee that large numbers of children will not only fail to learn but will be left far behind, if not driven out of the system altogether.

Our traditional system of locally controlled public education has not, by the stretch of anyone's imagination, been the best we could or should have. As we will see in more detail a bit later on, achieving genuine democratic educational quality requires not just abandoning the new standards-and-testing agenda but reconceptualizing our entire system of public schooling. To that end, we need briefly to revisit and clarify the major threats both to the present system and to the ultimately desirable system. Perhaps it is not so startling that at least two of these threats—charters and vouchers—have been proposed as highly democratic correctives to some of the widely perceived weaknesses of the traditional system of public education that has prevailed in this country since before it was a country.

The Trouble with Charters

It is true that charter schools are still technically public schools, and they do provide a growing number of parents with a degree of educational choice they often lack within their local districts. It is also true—and obviously beneficial—that most state charter legislation stipulates that charter schools may not be selective in their admissions policies and that their student bodies must be racially and ethnically representative of the districts in which they are located. And most charter schools do employ a nondiscriminatory lottery to determine admissions when the schools are oversubscribed.

However, the funding for almost all charter schools is not new money supplied by the state or federal government but money that is subtracted, per pupil, from the budget of the local school district or from total state aid going to local districts, thus reducing locally controlled public schools' funding. Also, charters unfortunately provide a convenient wedge by which for-profit corporations can enter the field of public schooling.

There have also been severe financial and managerial problems with some charter schools, both for-profit and nonprofit. Some have been forced to close, in many cases because of inadequate supervision by state education authorities. For instance, the *Boston Globe* recently reported that the for-profit firm Advantage Schools Inc. "misled parents about teacher qualifications, failed consistently to boost scores on high-stakes state tests, and engaged in financial practices that prompted censure by two states. Schools in four cities—Malden, MA, Chicago, Albany, NY, and Rocky Mount, NC—have ended their relationships with Advantage, in part over financial concerns."[16] The Massachusetts inspector general's office issued a study in November of 1999 of twenty-four charter schools, both nonprofit and for-profit, and reported finding financial and administrative "weaknesses that could undermine charter schools' ability to achieve their educational objectives and jeopardize the interests of state taxpayers."[17]

Last but hardly least, charter schools are too often not being allowed to fulfill one of their most important original purposes—to provide an opportunity for innovation, to explore new and improved ways of educating children and young people. These schools were conceived as being able to innovate because they were freed from all local district regulation and such stultifying district practices as teacher unions and contracts. But, like in-district pilot schools, charter schools in virtually every state are being required to operate within the educational straitjacket of mandatory curriculum standards and high-stakes standardized tests, thus eliminating any chance of genuine innovation or radical change.

The Trouble with Vouchers

One of the main dangers of the voucher movement is that voucher money in most cases is, again, not new state or federal money but money diverted from existing district funding, thus further impoverishing the district schools. The already inadequate funding for local district public schools, especially inner-city public schools, is being further eroded in order to favor the children of the relatively well off.

Also, voucher advocates have essentially given up on the public schools. To be fair, many of these advocates are genuinely concerned about the large numbers of inadequately educated inner-city poor and minority children. And despair on the part of the parents of those children—and the resulting desire to get their children into "good" schools by whatever means available—is perfectly understandable. However, if nonpoor, nonminority, non-inner-city advocates of vouchers are seriously interested in improving the educational lot of poor and minority inner-city children, why are they not advocating that this richest of all human societies repair or replace those ancient, crumbling inner-city school buildings? Why are they not advocating that we reduce classes of thirty-five or forty-five students to a more reasonable twenty or less, that we staff those schools with well-trained and well-paid teachers, that we supply those classes with up-to-date educational materials and electronic equipment? Why are they not advocating that we provide more than merely adequate support services to assist poverty-stricken children and their families, early childhood education for all young children being just one example, to say nothing about launching a major effort to repair and restore the communities in which they live?

The refusal of supporters of vouchers—many of them conservative, outright right-wing, and almost always well-off people—to advocate equalizing the educational opportunities we offer our poor and minority children and young people verges on the criminal, and their motives are often all too transparent. For example, it is possible that eventually middle- and upper-class students already enrolled in private schools could get vouchers to pay for part or all of their tuition. Then too, unless the Supreme Court delivers a First

Amendment–violation ruling in the voucher cases heading in its direction, vouchers could be used to pay for tuition to parochial schools that openly promote a particular religion. The Supreme Court has now accepted the Cleveland case, and a ruling is expected sometime in 2002.

Finally, will students who use vouchers receive a "better" education than they would receive in their public schools? There isn't much information to go on here. Because of the serious civil rights and financial questions, there have so far been few voucher programs for researchers to study, the main ones being the pilot projects in Milwaukee, Wisconsin, and in Cleveland. In any case, the research that has been done so far is both contradictory and inconclusive.[18] And, unfortunately, "better" education in these studies is always defined as improved scores on standardized tests, which is hardly the basis for making any sound judgment about so revolutionary a proposal as vouchers.

The voucher idea also has severe practical problems. The present nonpublic school system in this country educates only about 10 percent of the school-age population. If vouchers became widespread, the number of nonpublic schools would have to increase greatly. Most voucher plans—so far, at least—do not include the vast sums of money that would be required to create, staff, and house thousands of these new schools. Either the public treasury would be required to pay these start-up costs, or the new private schools would somehow have to take over the ancient, crumbling public school buildings and repair them, also at public expense.

Further, even the most generous voucher proposals so far offer no more than $2,500 (in Cleveland) to $4,000 a year, which does not begin to cover the tuition costs of most nonpublic schools, even relatively low cost parochial schools. Elite private schools, such as Phillips Exeter and Phillips Andover, cost roughly $20,000 per student per year. Where would the money come from to make up for shortfalls as large as this? Certainly not from the empty pockets of poor and minority parents.

There is also the intractable problem of accountability. Providing public tax money, even if it is routed to private and parochial schools through parents in the form of vouchers, would require some form of public accountability guaranteeing that the money is being spent wisely and honestly. There would also have to be guarantees that the nonpublic schools would obey all existing civil rights laws. For instance, they would no longer be able to discriminate in their admissions and retention procedures on the basis of race, religion, sex, ethnic group, or income level. Finally, if the tax-supported public schools must meet the demands of the high-standards-high-stakes-testing agenda, how could the now partly tax-supported nonpublic schools accepting voucher money be exempted from such demands?

The most vociferous opposition to vouchers will thus no doubt increasingly come from the nonpublic schools themselves. The appeal of these schools rests with at least three fundamentally antidemocratic differences from their public counterparts. First, they charge tuition and thus limit their clientele to those who are able to pay it—the middle and upper economic classes. Second, they can admit only students who are likely to measure up to their academic and behavioral standards. Last, they can get rid of their failures and troublemakers if by some mischance they admit them. How many private or parochial schools are willing to give up their ability to select the students they admit, to refuse to accept "difficult to educate" children and young people? How many of them will give up the ability to expel not only disruptive students but also students who fail to live up to the school's academic standards? And how many of them will be willing to give up the educational autonomy they now have and be subjected to the authoritarian rule of state standards and tests?

While voucher advocates are using the legitimate anguish of poor and minority parents to pry open the public coffers, their ultimate aim, one all too easily suspects, is to alter the traditional democratic—if most certainly not always achieved—aim of American public education, which is to serve all children and young people on a fair, just, and equal basis.

4

The Ominous Attempt to Privatize Public Education

When all these charter/voucher/anti–public school trends are taken into consideration, a sinister pattern emerges. What many of these advocates ultimately appear to want is a largely privatized, two-tier system of American education.

The charter school movement has provided an opening through which for-profit private corporations can infiltrate public education. While almost all charter schools must be incorporated as nonprofit entities and have a nonprofit board of directors or be sponsored by a nonprofit institution such as a college or university, in most states it is perfectly legal for these nonprofit entities to hire a profit-making private corporation to run the school. And private corporations are ready, willing, and all too able to take advantage of this opportunity.

The for-profit private sector, of course, has long had both feet in the business of public education. Private companies have traditionally created and supplied virtually all the textbooks and other curricular materials the public schools use and are now the recipient of enormous sums being invested in computers and other information technologies. Private companies such as the Educational Testing Service devise and market most standardized tests. Private companies also build and furnish all of our school buildings and run many food service, custodial, and transportation operations.

The Encroachment of the Private Sector

We are now witnessing a quite different phenomenon. Private corporations such as the Edison Project have been contracted not only to run charter schools

21

but also to run individual public schools and even entire school systems. There is also a growing movement to allow private companies to run publicly supported day-care and early childhood programs. And a burgeoning number of private companies have been set up to provide coaching and remedial services to students whose parents are rich enough to pay for them, thus creating even greater disparities in test results between the deserving rich and the undeserving poor.

But we are now moving into still newer territory. Visionary corporate and venture capital entrepreneurs are beginning to think seriously about transferring the corporately "successful" health maintenance organization model to the field of public education. Given the profits being made by HMOs since they have taken over the health-care system, businesspeople are now eager to create EMOs, or Educational Maintenance Organizations, to take over what they claim are our clearly failed and excessively costly public schools and school systems.

Should this happen, the field of public education would be subjected to the same kind of efficiencies and "cost containments" (and the resulting corporate "success") apparent in the privatized HMO health-care system. Educational decisions would be made not by principals and teachers in the schools but by remote corporate minions holding charts showing that special-help and remedial programs for learning disabled, special needs, and poor and minority kids don't meet the bottom-line cost-benefit analyses of the corporate managers. In other words, private enterprises would be greatly interested in being well paid to educate the relatively well off, the relatively easy (and less costly) to educate portion of the student population who would constitute the upper- or first-tier of a new two-tier educational system. But they would not be all that interested in funding the education of poor, minority, and special-needs students who would not be able to pay their EMO premiums. The families of most of "those kids" would not have supplementary "educational insurance" policies or benefit plans (except for whatever meager public, Medicare-like programs are available) to cover the EMO costs, and therefore their children would remain educationally uninsured right along with the forty million or so Americans who have no health insurance and who are therefore not eligible to join an HMO. "Those kids" would be compelled to remain in the second tier—a public educational system receiving even less money than it does now and therefore becoming an even greater educational disaster than it already is.

The Edison Example

The for-profit Edison Schools Corporation operates 113 public schools (about half of them charter schools) serving 57,000 students in 21 states and the District of Columbia and is seeking to add many more schools in cities like New

York and Chicago. One of Edison's major claims is that an Edison school, while receiving no more money per pupil than the public schools in its surrounding district, is guaranteed to outperform those schools in raising the standardized achievement test scores of its students and that all its students are virtually assured of passing the new state high-stakes tests.

The company also claims it will be able to make a profit—eventually (the Edison corporation lost forty million dollars in 2000). Company executives propose to do this by standardizing the managerial structure and the curriculum in all its schools, aiming that curriculum directly at the standardized tests the students will be taking, training teachers to teach to only that curriculum and those tests, and buying standard books, supplies, and equipment on a massive scale for all its schools all across the country. All Edison schools will thus essentially be clones of one another, with no significant variations or innovations allowed.

Does This Industrial Model Work?

Researchers at the Evaluation Center at Western Michigan University recently released a report examining the track record of ten of the schools Edison established during its first two years of operation—that is, schools that have been in business for at least four years and thus have had a reasonable chance to establish a track record. In conducting the study, the researchers defined educational "success" or "failure" in precisely the terms used by the Edison people themselves—scores on standardized tests.

"It is clear from our findings," says Dr. Gary Miron, a principal research associate at the center and one of the authors of the report, "that across all the schools we studied, Edison students do not perform as well as Edison claims. We looked at these ten schools because they were the Edison schools with the most years of data available for study. We evaluated student achievement in terms of gains Edison students made relative to comparison groups, as opposed to Edison's preference for evaluating gains made by the schools relative to themselves." While the schools did show some improvement from year to year on norm-referenced tests, interpreting these results was limited by the small number of students who could be traced from year to year in the data Edison provided.

"But," says Miron, "on criterion referenced tests—those that measure whether or not students meet prescribed state standards—Edison students' gains or losses mirror those of students in the comparison groups examined, which included students from the surrounding school districts."

The researchers overall conclusions were that "Edison student performance often lags behind district performance and almost always is below state performance levels" and that "while students in Edison schools often start out at levels below the national norms and district averages, they progress at rates comparable to students in other district schools. Unfortunately, this conclusion does not meet Edison's goal, which is to have achievement performance levels that exceed the levels of comparable schools."[19]

Over the past year or so Edison has suffered further defeats. For one, the San Francisco Board of Education voted to remove Edison from the management of one of its charter schools, citing bad management practices.[20] For another, Edison's bid to take over five "failing" New York City schools went down to defeat in 2001 when parents failed to vote in favor of the proposal.

According to an article in the *New York Times,* however, at least one Edison supporter did not see the New York defeat as a major calamity for the company—and he inadvertently revealed the basic problem with the entire privatization movement. In that article, Howard Block, a financial analyst at Banc of America Securities, in San Francisco, is quoted as saying that Edison was wise to pull out: "I wouldn't want to be managing schools in that city, with the constant media exposure and the politically charged atmosphere. *The amount of energy and resources needed are disproportionate to the size of the business opportunity there*"[21] (emphasis added). But it is precisely those "disproportionate" conditions that the berated and "failing" public educators must face and hope somehow to conquer every day of their working lives.

A Set of Fundamental Moral Questions

The idea of private-sector, for-profit schools raises some very important questions, not just relative to public education but to American society as a whole. When did it become morally acceptable in this American nation for private corporations to make enormous profits not only from educating the young in our public schools but also from caring for the sick in our health-care system and even from guarding and attempting to rehabilitate convicted criminals in our prisons? And when did it become the principal role of American public education to supply suitably trained and docile workers to staff the sectors of a business economy rather than to help students become productive, responsible citizens of a true democracy?

In the case of our public schools, the cause for concern goes well beyond whether private corporations should be allowed to make a profit from educating children rather than plowing that money back into improving the educational process. By their very nature and design private corporations in a capitalistic economy are not democratic institutions. Rather, despite all public relations rhetoric to the contrary, they are and must be hierarchical, top-down authoritarian entities devoted not to the accomplishment of broad, democratic social goals but to the narrow economic demands of profits and the bottom line. It is precisely the adoption of this authoritarian, hierarchical, antidemocratic, dehumanized corporate model that lies behind the "high" standards and "high stakes" testing agenda that is currently devastating our system of public education.

If any proof of this contention is required, we need only to look at the common, time-honored practices of our major corporations and businesses during an economic downturn or when a corporation is failing to do well even in a period of economic prosperity. The immediate response in these situations (such as the Enron catastrophe) is not to fire the CEO but to "downsize" the enterprise by laying off thousands of employees and throwing them to the economic wolves of unemployment, lost health benefits, and abandoned pension plans. In those cases where a CEO *is* fired for incompetence, he or she floats comfortably down to an early retirement on the billows of a golden parachute comprising an enormous pension and opulent stock options.

Must This Be the Future?

Where will this corporatization and privatization end? Already massive corporate conglomerates are taking over the entertainment and communications world of film, television, computers, and telecommunications. Conglomerate empires own and run our newspaper, book, and magazine publishing industries. The corrupting power of these same conglomerates is felt every day in our state houses, the halls of Congress, and the Oval Office as they extend their control over the political system through enormous campaign contributions and richly endowed lobbyists. And on and on.

These disheartening trends are simply additional manifestations of the move toward an American society that is not governed by the powerful humanitarian motives of caring for, protecting, and nurturing all of its people—and especially the young. This new society is ruled by the purely materialistic motives of the savage new global economic system and the unbridled rule of the huge, "lean and mean," "downsizing" multinational corporations that grow more powerful each day as they merge into macrocosmic entities that increasingly dominate the *entire world's* social, economic, and political order.

Who Is Doing This?

It is these corporate leaders (such as Louis Gerstner of IBM) who are playing the major role in the authoritarian, antidemocratic educational regime of high standards and high-stakes testing. They have had a heavy hand in assembling the impressive cast of largely self-appointed noneducational experts—state and local politicians and legislators, foundation executives, and department of education bureaucrats—who have attended the four national educational "summits" and declared that the new global economy requires the imposition of narrow, "world class" academic standards and equally narrow high-stakes testing.

The basis for those summits and the resulting standards-and-high-stakes-testing agenda has been the intellectually scandalous *A Nation at Risk* report issued by the U.S. Department of Education in 1984. This report falsely charged the nation's public schools with being "awash in a tide of mediocrity" and charged our students with falling further and further behind the other industrialized nations of the world on standardized school achievement test scores. This deterioration, said the report, seriously threatened the economic health and future condition of the nation.

Many attempts were immediately made and are still being made to point out that these charges are simply not true. This country's students do quite well in test-score comparisons with students in other countries, as has been repeatedly pointed out by Gerald Bracey, one of the leading experts in educational research and testing (two of his books are listed in the Bibliography). And the U.S. economy has somehow gone on to become the most powerful economic engine the world has ever seen.

As the eminent social and educational thinker Richard Rothstein has pointed out, when *A Nation at Risk* was issued in 1984 the economy appeared to be in big trouble. That report attempted to prove that this poor economic performance was the result of the shoddy quality of the country's public schools. In those days, the unemployment rate (and in many minds the *unemployability rate*) was over 6 percent and the school dropout rate twice that.

By the first year of the new millennium, the unemployment rate was 3.9 percent and even high school dropouts were finding jobs.[22] The American system of public education, however, was *not* being credited as a major cause of this economic miracle. And as we move further into the new century's first decade, that economic miracle turns out to have been an irrationally exuberant bubble, as many high-tech and dot.com companies have led the collapse into a recession and as thousands of employees are being laid off all over the country. And those obscenely overpaid CEOs and investment bankers who were behind the bubble and are now responsible for this downturn (along with the terrorists who devastated the country with their calamitous destruction of the Word Trade Center and a part of the Pentagon) are not only almost all well-educated graduates of four-year colleges and universities but also holders of advanced MBAs from prestigious business schools. Once again the "best and the brightest" are leading us down a primrose path, just as they did with the Vietnam War.

These same highly educated corporate leaders are also always searching for tax breaks and subsidies from the local communities in which they are located, threatening to pull up stakes and leave town for greener fiscal pastures in other communities offering even greater breaks. If they are building a new factory, they foment a competitive frenzy among local communities, who vie for those new jobs by offering tax breaks and free local services like roads and other infrastructures. Robert Reich, the former U.S. Secretary of Labor and now a professor of history and economic policy at Brandies University, has estimated that the tax breaks and subsidies offered to businesses and corporations by local communities in 1999 came to more than seventeen billion dollars. This is enough, he figures, to fund the education of one and a half million elementary school children at *double* the national average rate per pupil.[23]

And it is those same obscenely rich CEOs, those governors and state legislators, department of education bureaucrats, and foundation officials who have not held a fifth national education summit to announce that their highly touted reform agenda of high standards and high-stakes testing may be totally irrelevant to the economic performance of the nation and that, indeed, it may even be wrongheaded, educationally damaging, and economically counterproductive. Apparently they have dismissed the possibility that the sad economic conditions spelled out in *A Nation at Risk* and the disturbing economic downturn we are currently experiencing have both been caused by their own inept (and often corrupt) management practices.

5

"Dumbing Down" via Narrow Standards and High-Stakes Tests

The *Brown* decision and the United Nations' Declaration of Human Rights highlight two generally accepted aims of any truly high-quality, democratic system of education:

1. It must provide every child with a fully and equally funded desegregated education.
2. This education must be directed to the full development of each child's human personality and therefore fit the individual child's educational needs, talents, and interests.

The new national agenda of inflexible academic standards and high-stakes testing, while perhaps not as immoral as deliberate segregation, does nothing to meet either of these goals. It cares little about genuine educational quality and it is also inhumane, undemocratic, and therefore, many of us believe, unconstitutional.

The latest version of this agenda, proposed by the Bush administration and now passed by Congress, requires that every student in the United States be tested in every grade from 3 through 8 and that all students should show a certified (but not yet specified) degree of improvement every year. However, this legislation does *not* require that all private and parochial students be tested as well, thereby ensuring that the children of the wealthy—presumably including most members of the Bush administration and Congress, among many others—will not be subjected to the antieducational standards and testing regime that has prompted every state in the union except Iowa to impose a single standardized curriculum on all their public schools and therefore on all public school children and their parents.

Many of these new academic standards, according to the teachers, principals, and school administrators who must impose them, are hopelessly abstruse, excessively demanding, and quite inappropriate for the age and intellectual level of the children and young people who are forced to attempt to meet them.[24] Consider two examples selected at random by that foremost educational researcher Gerald Bracey[25]:

- A tenth-grade social studies standard in Virginia: "The student will analyze the regional development of Asia, Africa, the Middle East, Latin America, and the Caribbean in terms of physical, economic, and cultural characteristics and historical evolution from A.D. 1000 to the present."

- A sixth-grade standard from South Dakota: "Students will analyze the geographic, political, economic, and social structures of the early civilization of Greece with emphasis on the location and physical setting that supported the rise of this civilization; the connections between geography and the development of city-states, including patterns of trade and commerce; the transition from tyranny to oligarchy to early democratic patterns of government and the significance of citizenship; the differences between Athenian, or direct, democracy and representative democracy; the significance of Greek mythology in the everyday life of the people in Ancient Greece and its influence on modern literature and language; the similarities and differences between life in Athens and Sparta; the rise of Alexander the Great in the north and the spread of Greek culture; and the cultural contributions in the areas of art, science, language, architecture, government, and philosophy."

Similarly, here's a tenth-grade standard from the Massachusetts Comprehensive Assessment System (MCAS) History and Social Science Learning Standards:

> Interdisciplinary Learning: Natural Science, Mathematics, and Technology in History. Students will describe and explain major advances, discoveries, and inventions over time in natural science, mathematics, and technology; explain some of their effects in the past and present on human life, thought, and health, including the use of natural resources, production and distribution and consumption of goods, exploration, warfare, and communications.[26]

These are merely drops in the vast ocean of what is being required in every academic subject in the conventional academic curriculum. A study conducted by Mid-continent Research for Education and Learning has estimated that it would take twenty-two years of conventional schooling for any student to begin to meet all the standards in all the core subject areas being mandated by most states.[27]

Which is not to say that these things aren't worth knowing or that they aren't topics of interest to scholars in our colleges and universities. Nevertheless, serious questions must be raised—and are being raised—about whether such abstruse scholarly topics have any genuine relevance to the present and future lives of the vast majority of the students who are being subjected to them, even those who are headed for higher education.

This attempt to impose on all students an authoritarian, uniform, academically orthodox definition of what it is to be an "educated person" is being cemented in place by the imposition, in almost every state, of new, again "more rigorous" standardized pencil-and-paper (most often multiple-choice) tests that all students must pass before they can be promoted to the next grade and eventually graduate from high school. All public schools are now being forced to "align" their curricula with the tests—to teach to and only to the academic orthodoxy contained in and thus authorized by the standards and in most cases documented by a single high-stakes test.

The National Center for Fair and Open Testing (FairTest) and many other testing experts believe that the high-stakes tests currently in use are overlong, overly complicated, and academically unfair and inaccurate because they often test what has not yet been studied and are often set at levels well above the legitimate academic expectations for most students. And perhaps worst of all, these experts say, the tests—many of them multiple-choice tests requiring a student to select one right answer from four that are offered—require only the memorization and regurgitation of disconnected, unrelated facts rather than genuine intellectual thought.[28]

Here are some of the multiple-choice MCAS test questions based on the grade 10 history and social science learning standard quoted above[29]:

In fourteenth century Mali, the king and most of his court were:

A. Hindus
B. Christian
C. Jews
D. Muslims

Before 1800, which civilization most heavily influenced Japan?

A. Chinese
B. Russian
C. Greek
D. Arabian

The Industrial Revolution in England began with the manufacturing of:

A. Glass

B. Textiles

C. Steel

D. Paper

This last question is particularly interesting, since there is a great deal of scholarly dispute about the precise origins of that revolution. The test says the right answer is steel, but an equally powerful argument can be made for textiles (or for that matter, the steam engine). Most scholars would be quite reluctant to specify any single cause or starting point for so complex a historical event as the Industrial Revolution. Any attempt to so oversimplify history is patently ridiculous, antihistorical, and anti-intellectual, an excellent example of how a curriculum gets "dumbed down" as a result of mindless rote learning and multiple-choice testing.

According to FairTest, high-stakes tests are also often badly administered and in thousands of cases incorrectly scored. These testing malfeasances cause unjustified anguish and misery for thousands of children and their parents in all parts of our country.

Larry Myatt, principal of Boston's Fenway High School, the first of that city's "pilot" schools, which serves some three hundred inner-city students, says that 90 percent of Fenway's graduating seniors are admitted to an institution of higher education. However, a large number of those seniors also fail the state's tenth-grade MCAS exam that will determine whether they are awarded a high school diploma. In 2002, when that graduation requirement kicks in, Myatt says dozens of his best students may be admitted to college but will be unable to attend because they didn't pass the exam and get a high school diploma. Myatt believes that the MCAS exam will produce massive "'teaching only to the test'" and that it will end up rewarding those students who are best prepared only to take the test and punishing those who are prepared not only for college but also for work and the rigors of real life.[30]

States, meanwhile, are spending millions of scarce dollars on administering the tests, on developing new, higher standards in all subjects, on monitoring school district compliance, and on reporting results. Local districts are diverting large sums of money from classroom support in order to purchase test-preparation materials from private corporations in a desperate attempt to look good in the public eye.

In the case of most urban districts, this is a hopeless task. State education departments often release raw scores for individual schools and districts, ranking them with no accompanying qualifying information. These suspect and inaccurate test results are then trumpeted throughout the land by newspaper and television journalists who haven't done their homework. By some remarkable coincidence, the high-scoring schools and districts turn out to be the well-funded suburban schools and districts, while the low-scoring schools and districts are the ones serving poor, minority, special-needs, and limited-English-proficiency students.

For example, the Massachusetts MCAS tests are given to students in grades 4, 8, and 10. According to a statistical analysis conducted by Craig Bolon, the president of Planwright Systems, a software development firm:

> As in other states, Massachusetts and its newspapers and organizations review and publish test scores as though they were nearly exact, highly significant measures of school performance. A detailed analysis of results from the tenth-grade mathematics tests for academic high schools in metropolitan Boston showed that statistically they are not. Two factors describing characteristics of student populations explained about 80 percent of the variance among schools:
>
> - Average community income level, by far the dominant factor, and
> - Percentage of students with limited English proficiency, a weaker factor.
>
> Once contributions from these factors had been subtracted from test score averages for schools, the residual scores appeared to be statistical noise.... There is no credible evidence that changing test techniques can somehow cure the problems of state-sponsored student testing. Testing has become a cult, sanctimoniously promoted by large corporations to advance their own interests.[31]

Punishing Students for the Failure of Their Schools

According to a press release for *Raising Standards or Raising Barriers?*, a new book published by the Harvard Civil Rights Project, "the current overreliance on high-stakes testing threatens to deepen America's educational inequities.... Most of the contributors to [this] volume have found evidence that policies that focus on high-stakes testing corrupt educational reform and undermine achievement, especially for at risk students.... Congress has just voted to greatly expand mandated state testing, requiring the development of 213 additional state tests, the expenditure of billions of dollars, and the loss of a great deal of instructional time in schools all across the country. The time has come to hold the testing industry accountable and to ask what do we really know about the costs and benefits of testing. Too often we get poor tests which are misused to test things not taught and to punish the children attending inferior schools, violating basic concepts of fairness and civil rights."[32]

Nor is this new regime of excessively difficult standards and poorly designed tests the end of this sad story. In an effort to end what the school authorities call "social promotion," many schools "retain in grade" students who do not pass the tests. In Boston students who don't pass the eighth-grade state test are forced to go to summer school and then, if they still do not pass the test, are assigned to "transition" classes during their first year of high school. "This," says Judith Baker, a veteran Boston teacher in the city's Madison Park High School, "is the same exact thing as tracking used to be." The transition-class students

> are denied electives or creative programs, they take double English and math, and if they fail these, they will probably go into transition tenth-grade and eleventh-grade classes. . . . Although there is an attempt to bolster these courses, they are essentially remedial. They create "higher" and "lower" tracks just by taking the majority of entering ninth graders into what automatically becomes the school's "lower" track. These "transition" classes throw the entire curriculum sequence off, because they delay until later grades many required courses, and by the time students fulfill their requirements, they will *never* have had a chance to take an elective, an honors, or an AP course, anything remotely interesting. Students are responding by being sullen and bored, by failing (the guidance counselor for grade 9 went home with a shopping bag stuffed full of warning notices), and by exhibiting other negative behavior. I have heard of no positive behavior, academic or otherwise, associated with the "transition" course.[33]

The people at the Harvard Civil Rights Project also have a few words of condemnation about the use of high-stakes tests:

> Despite the political popularity of the testing "solution," many educators and civil rights advocates are suggesting that it has actually exacerbated the problems it sought to alleviate. They claim that these policies discriminate against minority students, undermine teachers, reduce opportunities for students to engage in creative and complex learning assignments, and deny high school diplomas because of students' failure to pass subjects they were never taught. They argue that using tests to raise academic standards makes as much sense as relying upon thermometers to reduce fevers. Most compellingly, they maintain these tests are directing sanctions against the victims rather than the perpetrators of educational inequities.[34]

No Surprises

What then are the utterly expectable results of this wave of "school reform"? The reformers say that "all children can and now will learn" if only they and their teachers "buckle down," work hard, and concentrate only on those lessons that will help them pass the tests and raise their test scores every year. Forget about the savage inequalities. Success can be achieved solely by hard work and by teaching only to the standards and the tests.

But it's no secret which students are going to fail these tests, and are already failing them all over the country. They are the poor and minority children and young people—especially those with no or limited English proficiency and those with special needs—who inhabit our savagely unequal schools (Madison Park High School, where Judith Baker teaches, has a student body made up almost entirely of minorities and children who qualify for free or reduced-price lunches).

As thousands of poor and minority children and young people continue to fail the tests and to be publicly excoriated as failures, they will believe the labels certifying them as failures, they will realize what that failure means in terms of their chances in life, and they will drop out of school as quickly as they legally—or illegally—can. According to recent Massachusetts Advocacy Center statistics, over the years 1995–1999, the period in which the high-stakes SAT-9 and MCAS testing programs have been in effect, Boston's annual dropout rate for all students has increased by 34 percent—28 percent for African Americans, 40 percent for Hispanics, 43 percent for Asians, and 37 percent for whites.[35]

One of the great mysteries here is how the proponents of rigid, "high," strictly academic standards and strictly academic high-stakes testing have been able to convince themselves—and then gone on to attempt to convince the public at large—that the cure for this massive student failure is to give these students additional and endless doses of the same educational medicine that has so manifestly failed them in the first place.

And it is not just the students who are being punished. When poor and minority public school children don't pass the tests, their teachers and principals are also labeled "failures" and threatened with losing their job or with their school's being "taken over" by the state and "reconstituted" to make sure that children do pass the tests. School administrators who can get rid of low-scoring failures by having them drop out have hit upon a sure way to guarantee that the test scores of their school and school district will go up and that their school and district will be considered a "success."

As Harold Howe II, a former U.S. Commissioner of Education and a lifelong champion of the civil rights of this nation's underprivileged children, has put it: "It will take years to sort out how best to measure the learning among America's least fortunate kids. In the meantime, we are holding inner-city schools hostage to the results of computer-corrected standardized tests, defining our children as test scores rather than human beings."[36] It is almost as if the high-standards-and-high-stakes testing agenda is specifically designed to further afflict the afflicted and further comfort the comfortable.

But Not Good for Anybody

But even the largely financially comfortable and most often suburban students who pass the tests are not receiving a good and proper education. I and many others (among them educators in these suburban communities) maintain that the narrow, authoritarian, uniform, "high standards," academically and politically orthodox definition of what it is to be an educated human being is no better for them than it is for an African American or Hispanic child growing up in East Harlem or Watts or Madison Park's Roxbury. Many parents and school officials in wealthy, normally high-scoring suburban communities throughout the country are rising in protest against the standards and tests.

Take, for instance, the Lexington, Massachusetts, school system, located in the wealthy suburban ring surrounding the core city of Boston. Like all Massachusetts school districts, Lexington must administer the state-mandated Massachusetts Comprehensive Assessment System (MCAS) tests based on state-mandated standards in reading and math, a program now its in third year of operation. The school system's administrators are seriously concerned about the effects of MCAS testing even though Lexington students, as expected, have done well on the tests when compared with their inner-city counterparts in Boston.

According to the February 8, 2001, edition of the town's newspaper, *The Lexington Minuteman*, the then superintendent of schools, Patricia Ruane, told the paper's reporter, "There's an interesting set of questions we as administrators have to face. Do we administer a test that we think is harmful to our children?" Diane Tabor, the system's director of education in grades 6 through 12, expanded on this point: "It's a moral dilemma. We're learning some information for helping children but only in the context of testing that has the potential to short circuit learning . . . and may do harm."

The conception of a school held by these administrators is "a learning community that emphasizes life engagement skills, multidisciplinary lesson plans, and individuality." As a result of the state's mandated system of standards and tests, that conception is giving way to one of a test-preparation factory characterized by the rote memory of facts and the standardization of curriculum. As Superintendent Ruane put it, "Thinking is messy. Deep thinking is even messier. If you are thinking superficially, you turn the whole school day into 'drill and kill.' So we're trying to keep things in perspective and not allow it to displace what we think are important learning experiences for our children."

The tests are causing great stress throughout the system. As Ruane puts it, "We're trying to broker the stress on principals, who are feeling tremendous stress. There's also a trickle-down effect on teachers. For instance, there is a lot of stress on fourth-grade teachers [the test is given in fourth grade]. You are going to see people not wanting to teach at grades where there's heavy-duty testing, where there is the tremendous pressure for children to get high scores on the tests."

Joanne Benton, the system's director of elementary education, is particularly worried about the students. "What I think is really sad is the stress being put on children. We want them to enjoy school. But how long are the tests—15 to 18 hours?" Ruane chimes in, "We don't want the kids feeling that level of stress and distress. It's the valuing of the child as a unique person with a unique voice that's important. And you don't get there with drill and kill."

An equally outspoken protest has emerged in the rich New York City suburb of Scarsdale. Parents of roughly one hundred eighth graders—a third of the class—have boycotted the state standardized testing system, saying that it has stifled creativity and forced teachers to abandon the very programs that have made the Scarsdale schools excel. They have the support of school officials, including members of the board of education and the superintendent of schools, Michael McGill. "Excesses of the standards movement," says McGill, "have promoted lockstep education. They've diverted attention from important local goals, highlighted simplistic and sometimes inappropriate tests, needlessly promoted similarity in curriculum and teaching. To the extent they've caused education to regress to a state average, they've undermined excellence."[37]

New York City teachers are also being forced to teach a uniform curriculum geared only to the standardized tests imposed by the state and the central school system bureaucracy. They are compelled to use "a highly organized approach to teaching" and are sometimes expected "to work according to a minute-by-minute script." As one of the school system's "mentor" teachers assigned to make sure that all teachers in any particular school building are following the prescribed script put it, "The beauty of these types of [highly scripted] programs is that you [as a teacher] don't have to think about it. Everything is spelled out for you. All you have to do is prepare for it."[38]

6

Making Our Educational System Truly Democratic

I t is an unfortunate fact that the American system of public schooling has never achieved its goal of being truly democratic. No matter how hard we have tried over the past three centuries, we have not yet succeeded in providing every child with a fair, just, and equal education, an education that meets every child's needs, talents, and desires.

Unequal Beginnings

When Thomas Jefferson proposed his early system of universal, publicly supported education for Virginia in the late eighteenth century, he called for every one of Virginia's twenty counties to establish schools to which every (white) citizen could send their (male) children free for three years to be taught the "basic" skills of "reading, writing, and arithmetic."

Once that minimal amount of practical, down-to-earth schooling was accomplished for these white males, Jefferson proposed that each school then select one boy "of best genius" whose parents were too poor to pay for any further education, who would then be sent free to each county's single grammar school. Here these incipient scholars would be taught the scholarly subjects of Greek, Latin, geography, and "the higher branches of numerical arithmetic."

"By this means," said Jefferson, "twenty of the best geniuses will be raked from the rubbish annually and be instructed at the public expense so far as the grammar schools go. At the end of six years' instruction, one half are to be discontinued (from among whom the grammar schools will probably be supplied with future masters); and the other half, who are to be chosen for the superiority of their parts and disposition, are to be sent and continued three years in the study of such sciences as they shall choose at William and Mary College. . . ."[39]

The sons of the rich would, of course, be going to the three-year schools, the grammar schools, and William and Mary (and later Jefferson's own University of Virginia) without running any academic gauntlet or being raked from the rubbish or experiencing any danger of being "discontinued" for purely financial reasons.

Since Jefferson, the history of public schooling in this country has essentially been the story of heroic attempts to provide greater and greater amounts of schooling to larger and larger segments of the American population—to women; to African American, Native American, Latino American, and all other immigrant children; to the handicapped; and so on. We experienced bursts of concern for the underprivileged and the badly educated during the latter part of the nineteenth century and especially during the heyday of progressive education in the 1920s and 1930s and then again in the 1960s and early 70s, during the great civil rights revolution and President Johnson's war on poverty. But it has always remained as it was in Jefferson's day—a system that has basically served the unequal social and economic structure of American society.

The Unequal Structure of Our Educational System[40]

The British psychologist Ken Richardson describes the operational and pedagogical structure of the educational systems of almost all countries in the industrialized world, including Britain and the United States, thus:

> The education system is in many ways a pivot of the intellectual and class structure of the whole society. [Every] year groups of children appear to enter the system as a more or less homogeneous beam of light into a prism, and emerge as a spectrum of social classes reproducing that [spectrum as it exists] in the society from which they come. To most people this seems to be a natural process. In the twentieth century, schooling has come to be seen by almost everyone as the ultimate test of intelligence. To the general public, the perception of school is that of an objective and fair natural selection process, in which children, and their innate potentials, get sorted out by being asked to learn a neutral curriculum.
>
> The reality, of course, is much different. First, children enter school already advantaged or handicapped by the social inheritance of preconceptions of their own likely abilities.

Poor children, says Richardson, have already been "told" by their early environment and by the way their schools are run that nothing much intellectually is expected of them.

> The learning is far from neutral. The usual school curriculum, unfortunately, is the opposite of any socially meaningful context for learning. Children are not asked to learn the matters governing the lives of their parents and communities; the laws of motion of the local and national economy; the management of resources, people, and processes within them; local and national political administration; the structure and functions of institutions, and so on. Instead, they are asked to learn "subjects," which may seem fair enough, except that most of the subject matter that children learn in schools is not knowledge as we know it in scholarly circles, or as it is used in practical contexts. It comes in detached forms, specially packaged to suit the administrative constraints of school, and, of course, the ideological preconceptions of [society].

The "learning" that is then used as "evidence" of children's "innate" intelligence is, says Richardson, "of a very peculiar and moribund kind." School learning "involves, in the main, large amounts of fragmented information to be committed to memory; basic communication and computation (which children could probably learn more easily in wider contexts, anyway); and certain forms of knowledge classification." Richardson refers to this system as the "squirrels and nuts" theory "whereby young people bury endless chunks of information in their memories in case it might just come in useful some day."

Richardson also quotes the eminent cultural (and educational) psychologist Jerome Bruner as pointing out how schooling in which "children are subjected to artificial, made-up subjects that are not embedded in cultural practice . . . renders school learning tedious and irrelevant."

While agreeing that human intelligence may have an as yet undetermined and undeterminable genetic component, Richardson goes on to say that such intelligence in any individual human child "will fully develop only if keyed into or hooked up to external cultural tools. This is what our brains and cognitive system have been prepared for in the spectacular leap in evolution from apes to humans."

By cultural tools Richardson means "not just hardware and technological tools, but all of the economic and administrative institutions through which our complex societies operate. Being fully intelligent means having access to, and cognitive grasp of, those cultural tools, and the powers through which they operate. This doesn't mean that everyone should become directors of companies and financial houses, government ministers, or directors of education and social services. But it does mean that everyone should have a clear understanding of the deliberations and operations of those institutions, and how they can have a say in them and are affected by them. And it also means that individuals [should not be] restricted from fullest participation in them at all levels."

The educational environment that Richardson is describing here is the one the great developmental psychologist and educational reformer Seymour Sarason has been advocating for the past forty years (see his works listed in the bibliography): the creation in our schools of what he calls "contexts of productive learning," the transformation of those "tedious and irrelevant" educational experiences into experiences that "start where the students are" and move on from there, experiences in which children and young people can connect what they are learning with both what is going on inside themselves and what is happening out in the real world of their everyday lives.

These eminent educational thinkers are saying that while there may be some mysterious genetic element involved, human "intelligence" is developed only through educational activity that is based on and connected to the real world of everyday social and cultural life. Intelligence, in short, is not so much a *thing* as a *behavior*. It is not something we *possess* but something we *do*.

It is precisely the refusal of our present system of public schooling to base itself on the exercise of genuine intelligence in the real cultural world that has rendered the system so disconnected from the real lives of its students and thus so ineffective. So long as all children and young people are subjected to a schooling (and testing) process in which the learning is as unproductive as Richardson has described, no child or young person will receive an education that is going to do justice to that child's range of native abilities and legitimate social and cultural aspirations.

The Great Myth of High Test Scores and Good Jobs

What is perhaps most distressing and unconscionable about the high-standards-and-high-stakes-testing agenda is precisely that it is not preparing *any* of our students for the world they will be living in, not even for the jobs that may or may not be available in the corporate world. As Robert Reich has put it:

> Jobs in the old mass production economy came in a few standard varieties: research, production, sales, clerical, managerial, professional. A system that depended on economies of scale didn't need many specialized skills. Nor did it need much original thinking. Most people spent most of their working lives performing the same operation over and over, in the company of many other people who performed the same or similar operations. A standardized

education was appropriate because jobs were standardized. In general, the largest pedagogical challenge was to train young people to sit still for long periods of time, be patient, follow directions, and be punctual. These were the core competencies that industry required. . . .

But the old mass production system is disappearing. Computers, the Internet, and digital commerce have exploded the old job categories into a vast array of new niches, creating a kaleidoscope of ways to make a living. Musicians, artists, writers, and performing artists are discovering multimedia outlets for their talents. . . . Success in any of these jobs doesn't depend on the mastery of one uniform body of knowledge as measured by standardized tests. Quite the opposite. Most of the work in the emerging economy requires an ability to learn on the job, to discover what needs to be known, and to find and use it quickly.

Many of the new jobs depend on creativity—on out-of-the-box thinking, originality, and flair. Almost by definition, standardized tests can't measure these sorts of things. . . .

Our new obsession with standardized tests runs exactly counter to the new demands of the modern economy. It is training a generation of young people to become exquisitely competent at taking standardized tests, and a generation of teachers to become extremely good at teaching how to take them. Neither of these competencies has much to do with preparing young people for what they will encounter when they leave our schools.

The more disturbing prospect is that all the testing may have the opposite effect—dulling young people's interests in learning and dimming their creative sparks at a time in history when learning and creativity are more important to the economy than ever before.[41]

The "Problem" of Higher Education

One of the factors that governs and tends to rigidify our present unjust system of "lower" education—or at least one of the cries of frustration constantly heard from innovative elementary and high school educators—is the control that the colleges and universities exert over what can be done in our elementary and secondary schools. Many public K–12 educators see the perceived requirements for college admission, including the Scholastic Assessment Tests (SATs), College Board examinations, grade-point averages, and Carnegie units in compartmentalized subject areas, as a curricular and pedagogical straitjacket that effectively prohibits significant innovation.

This situation is even worse now that "high," strictly academic standards in these compartmentalized subject areas, along with high-stakes tests, are being instituted. It is almost as if we expect *every* child and young person to pursue a course of higher education, no matter how irrelevant such schooling might be to the needs, talents, and interests of that individual.

It has never, of course, been the intention of our institutions of higher education or of American society that *all* children and young people should be admitted to and graduate from a four-year college or university. Just the opposite. Given that the entire K–16 (and beyond) educational system is Richardson's pivot of the intellectual and class structure of the society as a whole and is designed to reproduce the spectrum of social classes as it presently exists, the majority of children and young people are *excluded* from going to an elite, four-year college or university. That privilege is restricted to those favored few who can successfully qualify as winners in our carefully rigged K–12 educational marathon.

Those winners have largely been and are still going to be nonminority middle- and upper-class students, most often suburban offspring of parents who have themselves run well in the educational race. Those parents are not going to support—much less insist on—radically innovative education in their public schools that might jeopardize their children's admission to "first class" colleges and universities.

But, of course, our system or postsecondary education is not limited to elite four-year colleges and universities. There are a broad range of these institutions, including state and regional colleges, technical institutes, and two-year community colleges. These institutions and the education they offer, however, are all too after considered "second class" in our hierarchical society, and they are no more prone to radical innovation than their four-year elite counterparts.

Is Change in the Air?

Despite the high-academic-standards agenda and especially the adoption in many states of a single high-stakes test to determine whether young people can receive a high school diploma and thus be eligible for college, none of the Ivy League colleges and universities nor most of their publicly supported counterparts would nowadays dream of using any single measure such as a test score to determine whether students are to be admitted—or permitted to graduate.

According to the *New York Times,* even when the venerable, revered, and discriminatory SATs and College Boards are used, institutions like Wesleyan University will "weigh a student's race, ethnicity, home town, as well as course selection, athletic prowess, alumni connections, artistic skill, musical talent, writing ability, community service, and the quality of the school" from which the student comes. These institutions want to make sure that their entering classes are "not only academically sound and ethnically and racially diverse but also well stocked with poets, running backs, activists, politicians, painters, journalists, and cellists." And these non-test-score criteria often lead to choosing students who have *lower* test scores than other applicants.[42]

Also, to the range of sterling and necessary human endeavors that are possibly *but not necessarily* enhanced by going to college, we need to add the full range of technical and mechanical skills, few of which are going to be acquired or honed by attending a four-year, strictly academic institution of higher learning. Just as we need poets, running backs, and cellists, we also need skilled, thoughtful, and equally well paid carpenters, electricians, plumbers, sheet metal workers, auto mechanics, construction workers, chefs, and so on, as well as skilled and not-so-skilled service workers. After all, it is the skilled and unskilled workers, many of them with only a high school education or less, who keep the social and economic worlds working.

So perhaps the world of higher education is beginning to move in a more inclusive, more democratic direction, a direction that could encourage rather than repel innovation.

Beating Down the SATs

Indeed, in part as a result of the growing revolt against standardized testing, many of our colleges and universities are abandoning or planning to abandon the SATs and those revered College Board exams as necessities for admittance. The president of the University of California, Dr. Richard C. Atkinson, has proposed that California's public university system abandon the SAT I as an admission criterion as soon as possible and eventually to phase out the College Board exams as well. "Simple fairness," says Atkinson, tells him that using the SAT I "is wrong. We are, after all a society built on twin notions: first, that actual achievement should be what matters most, and second, that people should be judged on the basis of what they have made of the opportunities available to them. Therefore, it seems only right that college-bound students should be judged on what they have accomplished during four years of high school, not on the basis of a single standardized exam designed to test undefined notions of 'aptitude.' "

He proposes that for the moment the university system continue using the SAT IIs in writing and mathematics and a third test of each student's choice until better and fairer tests can be developed. He would then also get rid of the SAT IIs.

But he sees the elimination of high-stakes standardized tests as "only a first step. We should also adopt a more comprehensive 'holistic' admissions process that takes a range of factors into consideration, from the quality of a student's high school to the opportunities available to the student. A young person who has made exceptional progress in challenging circumstances needs to be given special attention." He apparently is looking hard for those poets, running backs, activists, politicians, painters, journalists, and cellists.

Atkinson decries the SATs for their detriment "not just in the lives of students, but for teachers, parents, admissions officers, and university presidents. Parents who can afford it enroll their children in SAT preparation courses, now a $100 million per year industry. Teachers are under increasing pressure to raise students' scores. College admissions officers are also under pressure to increase the SAT scores of each entering class. . . . In short, it has become the educational equivalent of a nuclear arms race."[43]

This growing nonreliance on test scores and the inclusion in higher education of a wide range of talents and interests hitherto neglected spells out the kind of broad, inclusive, all-encompassing education we should offer all of our students and therefore the criteria we should be using in assessing the progress of those students as they move from kindergarten through high school.

What Should Our Schools Be Doing?

Any revolutionary changes in higher education will require an equal rethinking of elementary and secondary education, almost certainly as a joint effort. A dramatic example of how this can be done is the path-breaking study conducted in 1991 and 1992 by the Institute for Education in Transformation at the Claremont, California, Graduate School when faculty members became dissatisfied with what they themselves were doing.[44] They wanted, they said,

> to reconnect our graduate education programs with the real life of the schools, to get outside the ivory tower and look at the daily issues that confront students, teachers, administrators, and support staffs inside the public schools of this nation. For us, these projects began as an effort to make our own graduate education programs more relevant, particularly our graduate teacher education internship program. Through our daily work in teacher education and inside schools, it became increasingly clear that there was a tremendous gulf between life inside schools and the perceptions of that life by academicians, policy makers, media, and community leaders.

Leading members of the graduate faculty were also not happy with the various "educational reform" reports over the past twenty or so years, beginning with *A Nation at Risk.* While agreeing that a "crisis" did exist in the schools, they were not sure that the report researchers and writers were correct in identifying the basic problems with modern American schooling as being "the serious problem of student underachievement [and students dropping out], [the problem] that there are many children whose home environments make learning difficult, [the problem] that a significant number of teachers are not adequately trained in today's conditions, and [the problem] that these problems and others are exacerbated by the changes that have been, and still are, taking place in the general society outside of our schools."

Based on the very preliminary research they had been conducting inside schools, "it was our experience that the best educational practitioners were those most disappointed by these reports, not because they did not believe there was a crisis, but because these reports either missed critical issues or named problems that were only marginally related to those experienced inside schools."

In order to explore these questions more profoundly, the researchers designed a collaborative, participatory research project to name and describe the real problems of schooling from the inside, a project whose active researchers were the people living and working inside four typical California elementary and secondary schools—the students, teachers, day-care workers, custodians, secretaries, cafeteria workers, school nurses, bus drivers, administrators, parents, security guards, and counselors. These insiders would define the problems, conduct the research, and assess the results; the university staff would merely organize and assist.

The four schools selected for the study "had the profile of many schools in this country—low standardized test scores, in middle to lower socioeconomic areas, with students from multiple ethnic and linguistic groups, and faculties who (with the exception of one school that was new) had been in place many years and were largely Euro-American."

The school insiders spent a full year, holding over 160 meetings and four retreats, gathering twenty-four thousand pages of transcriptions, essays, drawings, journal entries, and notes, eighteen hours of videotapes, and eighty hours of audiotapes. Only after going through that full year and then spending another six months assessing their findings were they ready to make those findings public.

As the university teachers put it, "no one was more surprised by the results of this report than those of us on the outside. We, like the authors of previous reports on schooling and teacher education, would have predicted issues such as what to teach, how to measure it, how much a teacher knows, and choice of school would have surfaced; they did not. . . . Indeed, we fear that much of what academicians and policymakers now suggest for the improvement of our schools may actually complicate and exacerbate the problems identified here. At best, their suggestions may not change the situation inside classrooms at all."

The report begins by noting one interesting fact and one overall conclusion. The interesting fact is that over the eighteen months "the adult participants increasingly understood and came to agree with their students' perceptions of what was wrong with the schools," including one student's devastating statement that "this place hurts my spirit." The overall conclusion was, "Currently, the education system in the U.S. is one in which deeply committed people inside schools feel incapable of acting on their own values. The result is that participants inside schools, from students to administrators, feel unable to meet responsibilities, expectations, and goals for themselves and for others."

The report then laid out the seven basic issues uncovered in the course of the study, none of which involved low academic achievement, dropping out, poor home environments, inadequately trained teachers, or changes that have been, and still are, taking place in the general society outside the schools. Rather, the real underlying issues (in condensed form) were:

1. *Relationships.* The participants felt that the crisis inside schools is directly linked to human relationships and the barrenness, the poor quality, of those relationships. Everyone wanted relationships with individuals who care, listen, understand, respect others, and are honest, open, and sensitive. Teachers reported that "their best experiences in school are those where they connect with students and are able to help them in some way. They also report, however, that there is precious little time during the day to seek out individual students. Students also notice teachers' lack of time to speak to them individually. Parents say they want an honest dialogue between themselves and their children's teachers. Even more important, many parents fear that poor relationships between teachers and their children damage their children's sense of confidence and vitality. . . . When relationships in schools are poor, fear, name calling, [and] threats or incidents of violence, as well as a sense of depression and hopelessness, exist. This theme was prominently stated by participants and so deeply connected to all other theses in the data that it is believed this may be one of the two most central issues in solving the crisis inside schools."

2. *Race, culture, and class.* "Many students of color and some Euro-Americans perceive schools to be racist and prejudiced, from the staff to the curriculum. Some students doubt the very substance of what is being taught. . . . Many students in public education, especially but not exclusively students of color, are raised in poverty, also creating a myriad of mismatches with school design and expectation. Their prior experiences are often not understood by teachers whose personal experiences have been very different."

3. *Values.* While many people think that people of color and/or poor people in general hold different basic values from those of the dominant culture, "our data hold no evidence that people inside schools have significantly different fundamental values. Our data suggest that parents, teachers, students, staff, and administrators of all ethnicities and classes value and desire education, honesty, integrity, beauty, care, justice, courage, and meaningful hard work. . . . However, very little time is spent in classrooms discussing these issues and a number of restrictions exist against doing so."

4. *Teaching and learning.* "Students, especially those past fifth grade, frequently report that they are bored in school and see little relevance of what is taught to their lives and their futures. Teachers feel pressured to teach what is mandated and sometimes doubt the appropriateness for their students. Teachers also are often bored by the curriculum they feel they must teach. . . . Students from all groups, remedial and advanced, high school to elementary, desire both rigor and fun in their schoolwork. They express enthusiasm about learning experiences that are complex but understandable, full of rich meanings and discussions of values, require their own action, and those about which they feel they have some choice. According to student descriptions of the most boring and least relevant schoolwork, they include activities which stick closely to standardized materials and traditional transmission teaching methods. Students want more participation in important choices inside classrooms. Teachers feel a need for time to rethink curriculum and instruction and to form honest dialogues with one another regarding teaching. A good deal of knowledge about how to make teaching better already exists, but there is little time to learn or share such knowledge. Many of the students of color bring knowledge from their communities that they do not see represented inside school curriculum. This makes them doubt the curriculum and not feel validated."

5. *Safety.* "Related to disconnected relationships and not knowing about one another's differences is the issue of safety. Very few participants on campus or parents feel schools are safe places. Teachers, students, and staff fear physical violence. The influence of drugs, gangs, and random violence is felt by students. . . . An alarming number of our elementary students in an economically depressed area feel they may not live to be adults."

6. *Physical environment.* "Students want schools that reflect order, beauty, space, and contain rich materials and media. The desire for clean, esthetically pleasing and physically comfortable space is expressed by all."

7. *Despair, hope, and the process of change.* "Many participants feel
a hopelessness about schools that is reflected in the larger society and in
the music and art of our youth. Paradoxically, hope seemed to emerge
following honest dialogues about our collective despair. Participants are
[eager] for change and willing to participate in change they see as relevant.
We have strong indications that change inside schools might best be
stimulated through participatory processes. In these self-driven research
processes, participants come openly to discuss their hopes and dreams.
Through this process, we understood that there were shared common
values around which we could begin to imagine a more ideal school."

On What Should Students Be Assessed?

These Claremont results spell out the broad range of criteria we should be
using when we attempt to devise systems for "assessing" whether our schools
are succeeding in being what they should be and doing what they should be
doing and whether they are being held sufficiently "accountable" for the time,
effort, and money we are spending on them, even if that time, effort, and
money are at this present time manifestly insufficient for the task.

Yes, students in today's society need to be able to grasp and make use
of our abstract symbolic systems—they need to learn to read with skill and
pleasure and thus be able to acquire new knowledge, to be able to write clearly
and thus communicate more widely than from person to person, and to do
the elementary arithmetic required by everyday transactions.

However, not *every* student needs to learn algebra or the other higher
branches of mathematics or to study the novels of Dickens or even all of the
plays of Shakespeare. For instance, I was forced to take high school math
(in a school that was a clone of an all-male, all-white English "public" school)
through algebra, trigonometry, and solid geometry, hating and quickly forget-
ting every minute of it. I never did grasp algebra despite one-on-one tutoring,
and I have never been called on to use it or any of my other mathemati-
cal nonaccomplishments at any time since graduating from high school and
college. What I "learned" in school about mathematics was that it was something I hated, something I was simply too stupid too learn, and therefore something to be avoided at all costs. This is the great danger of all conventional,
top-down, authoritarian instructional schooling, especially when combined
with impossibly high academic standards and cruel high-stakes testing. What
it teaches children and young people is that all those wonderful things we
are supposed learn to love become dreary school "subjects" drilled into us
primarily so that we can be tested on them and be labeled school "successes"
rather than miserable failures.

I am not proud of being a phobic math illiterate. I resent what I am sure (or at least I hope) was simply bad teaching rather than innate logico-mathematical stupidity, since I'm also sure there are wonderful things to be experienced through a genuine love of mathematics. For while I may be a math phobe, I am a passionate pursuer of many other fascinating topics—not because I studied them in "school" but because I came across them or became reacquainted with them after leaving school. Among them are human evolution, the rise of the ancient Mesopotamian empires, the creation of the U.S. Constitution, the ballets of George Balanchine and Jerome Robbins, Classical Greece, the paintings of Michelangelo and Monet, the plays of (yes) Shakespeare, and the music of Bach, Handel, Mozart, and Henry Purcell.

Despite my passion for these great human achievements, I do not think that *every* student should be compelled to study and be tested on them whether they are ready to appreciate them or not just because I and many other people happen to be fascinated by them and believe them to be of great cultural importance. Indeed, I fervently wish that rather than being subjected to what for me were the horrors of algebra and trigonometry, I had instead been exposed at an earlier age and in the proper non-"instructional" ways to all of those things by which I might have been truly captivated. In my wildest nightmares, I often have visions of a young Mozart being forced to wrestle with algebraic equations rather than being free to write his symphonies, operas, divertimenti, and string quartets. Or a young Leonardo da Vinci forced to learn Latin and Greek so that he could converse with his humanistic contemporaries rather than dropping out of school and wandering the countryside sketching and observing nature. Or a young Shakespeare being encouraged to leave Stratford to continue his study of the classics at Oxford and become a learned don rather than fleeing to London to become an actor and playwright.

All students, of course, should have the opportunity to *explore* and come to love all of the great cultural possibilities, including algebra and higher mathematics. And in the course of their twelve years of schooling they need to explore and acquire those fundamental skills of reading, writing, and basic numbering—always assuming that these necessary skills are developed in students and therefore taught in ways that enable them to practice such skills in later life with pleasure rather than pain.

The developmental psychologist Howard Gardner describes what all too often happens in our schools when they pursue the traditional forms of strictly academic schooling divorced from Richardson's "cultural tools" ("all of the economic and administrative institutions through which our complex societies operate"). In these instances, says Gardner, "a pervasive antagonism often develops between the school's logical, out-of-context knowledge system and that practical participation in daily activities fostered informally by the culture. If this antagonism is to be lessened, schools . . . must be viewed as comfortable and significant environments, rather than hostile providers of useless knowledge. This means that schools must contain everyday life within their walls, while also revealing the relation between the skills they teach and the problems children find significant."[45]

What we need to do, as Gardner, Richardson, and the Claremont study so eloquently tell us, is to see whether we can turn our schools into *friendly providers of useful knowledge.* As Mihaly Csikszentmihalyi, Kevin Rathunde, and Samuel Whalen put it in their book *Talented Teenagers,* "The problem with our technologically inspired views of education is that we have come to expect learning to be a function of the rationality of the information provided. In other words, we assume that if the material is well organized and logically presented, students will learn it. Nothing is further from the fact. Students will learn only if they are motivated. The motivation could be extrinsic—the desire to get a well-paying job after graduation—but learning essential to a person's self must be intrinsically rewarding. Unless a person enjoys the pursuit of knowledge, learning will remain a tool to be set aside as soon as it is no longer needed. Therefore we cannot expect our children to become truly educated until we ensure that teachers know not only how to provide information but how to spark the joy of learning."[46]

Or as Gardner has also said:

> The single most important contribution education can make to a child's development is to help him toward a field where his talents best suit him [or her], where he [or she] will be satisfied and competent. We've completely lost sight of that. . . .
>
> We should spend less time ranking children and more time helping them to identify their natural competencies and gifts and cultivate those. There are hundreds and hundreds of ways to succeed and many, many different abilities that will help you get there.[47]

The Educated Human Being Redefined

I and many others are beginning to believe that the established and, indeed, entrenched academically orthodox definition of what it is to be an "educated person" is too archaic, too narrow, too confining, and too intellectually and socially counterproductive to be the basis for any truly democratic educational system aimed at meeting the demands of the enormously complex human society of the twenty-first century.

Rather, we should be concentrating our efforts on creating—both inside and outside our schools—Richardson's "socially meaningful context for learning" and Sarason's "contexts for productive learning." Through an educational system like this children and young people should be able to achieve Richardson's "clear understanding of the deliberations and operations of those institutions, and how they can have a say in them and are affected by them." And individuals would be able to participate in these institutions fully, at all levels.

The "educated person" who would emerge from a truly reformed system of education based on the schools outlined in the Claremont Study would not simply be a person who had succeeded in getting good grades in some narrow, disconnected, strictly academic curriculum, thereby landing in the upper reaches of some bell-shaped curve, a student who was able to pass a number of narrow, disconnected, strictly academic paper-and-pencil tests and be admitted to college. Rather, an "educated person" would be a human being with *all* of his or her inborn capacities fully developed, an intellectually, socially, artistically, and morally cultivated citizen able to understand and care about what is happening in the larger world, able to see what is still very much wrong with that world and how he or she might be able to contribute to making that world a better, more truly democratic, more humane place for *all* its inhabitants.

7

Providing Diversity and Choice

The article of the United Nations' Declaration of Human Rights guaranteeing parental choice is based upon two stubborn, important facts. The first is that children and young people do not come in any single size, shape, or collection of attributes, capacities, talents, and intelligence. The second is a corollary: there thus cannot be any single educational environment, any single set of academic standards, any single uniform curriculum, or any single standardized test—or, for that matter, any single battery of pencil-and-paper tests—that is going to be suitable and appropriate for all children. As Susan Ohanian puts it, "one size fits few."[48]

Just as there is a broad diversity among children and young people, there is an equivalent diversity of educational philosophies, curricula, and methodologies. Despite our growing scientific knowledge about how children and young people can best go about the task of learning and developing (as evidenced by the work of Richardson, Bruner, Gardner, and a host of other researchers), there is as yet no agreement among all parents and all professional educators on a one best way to achieve that "full development of the human personality."

In no small measure this lack of agreement is the result of the massive failure of those of us in education—especially higher education—to acquaint both ourselves and the general public with the scientific evidence amassed over the past fifty years in the fields of cognition and human development that clearly points to the educational correctness of the developmental approach to schooling. But even if such knowledge was widely known and accepted, there would still be room for a wide variety of differing educational arrangements. In any truly democratic society it is never morally permissible for *anyone* arbitrarily and dictatorially to impose any one-and-only way to educate children on all parents, all professionals, and all schools, no matter how solidly backed by scientific evidence.

It makes no difference how much I or anyone else believes that his educational philosophy and pedagogical approach is the right one for all children and young people. No one has or should have the power to impose his or her educational view on everyone else. It is therefore most certainly not the province of any federal government, any state government, or even any local school district to so impose a single way of educating all children and young people on all students, parents, and teachers.

Once again, just the opposite. It is very much the province and duty of the federal, state, and local educational establishments to make sure that all parents and professionals are presented with the full range of educational possibilities from which they may choose the one they believe is best for the children in their care. Those of us who accept the scientific evidence upholding the wisdom of a developmental approach to education devoutly hope, of course, that this approach will eventually become the widely instituted way of educating children. But this will have to come about because that approach proves its worth in the free marketplace of ideas and practice, not through undemocratically imposing it on an as yet unconvinced public.

Building a Constituency

The basic operating rule of most of our local school districts has historically been that all schools should be roughly similar to one another, that one size really does really fit all. During the 1960s and 70s a degree of diversity and parental choice was created in public education, primarily in our urban schools, as the result of desegregation and the creation of educationally diverse "magnet" schools that students could attend voluntarily. This diversity is now being seriously eroded—if not eliminated—by the uniform-standards-and-standardized-testing juggernaut that is selling the public on the idea that it is educationally and morally legitimate to impose a single, standardized curriculum and standardized testing on all of our schools and thus forcing all schools to become clones of one another.

The most immediate problem therefore is how we can best build a broad, grass-roots constituency for a system of American public education based on the democratic principles of educational diversity and parent/professional choice. If we are able to build such a constituency, we will then be able to force the corporate world, the U.S. Congress, and our state legislatures to abandon their autocratic agenda of antieducational and unconstitutional mandates.

Once the idea of and the desire for diversity and choice reaches a critical mass and has been established in the minds of both the parents and the educators of this country, we will have made it politically possible for our local school boards and central administrations to refuse to adopt the uniform standards and administer the uniform tests. If a sufficient number of local districts take part in such a boycott, there is no way the state and national authorities can avoid reconsidering what they are doing. It is only through the creation of such a powerful grass-roots movement that we will be able to reverse the undemocratic educational dementia from which we currently suffer.

The Rationale for Diversity and Choice

The reasons for creating and practicing educational diversity have been elo- quently stated by Seymour Fliegel, a former deputy superintendent in New York City's Community District 4, located in distinctly underprivileged East Harlem:

> The aim of [District 4] has been to create a system that—instead of try- ing to fit students into some standardized school—has a school to fit every student in this district. No kid gets left out, no kid gets lost. Every kid is important, every kid can learn if you put him or her in the right envi- ronment. But since kids have this huge range of different needs, different interests, and different ways of learning, we've got to have a wide diversity of schools.[49]

Creating broadly diverse new schools instead of attempting to change or reform existing schools is one of the most crucial aspects of District 4's revolution. As Deborah Meier, the creator of District 4's Central Park East schools, puts it, "Such new schools are important because it takes six generations to change existing schools and we haven't got time for that."[50]

As anyone who has attempted to transform an already existing nonchoice, nonmagnet, noncharter neighborhood school can testify, doing so is virtually impossible. Students attend because they happen to live within the school's designated attendance area. Almost all the teachers and administrators have been assigned there by central administration or have transferred there in search of an ill-defined greener pasture. They can't even agree on what the school's existing mission is, much less band together to create a radically new and different one.

Meier, Fliegel, and other District 4 people are advocating that every local school district, by continually creating new schools, gradually replace *all* of its existing nonchoice schools with new choice schools, each having a clear and shared sense of its educational mission. According to Meier:

> We need schools of choice for all children and parents, first as a means toward family/school trust. A system of choice offers a way of providing for increased professional decision making without a power struggle. Schools of choice—if they are small schools—can offer vastly more time for parents, teachers, and students to meet together—a practice that should be ensured by legislation mandating employers to provide time off for parents attending school meetings.
>
> Schools cannot accomplish this collective task without the support and trust of the student's family. Such trust is not a luxury. Young people sent to school with a message of distrust for the motives and methods of the school are crippled. They must step warily around what the teacher says, looking for hidden traps. Teachers, too, send out mixed messages: on the one hand if you don't behave I'll tell your mother, and on the other the values of your family won't get you anywhere.
>
> Teachers rate "parental indifference" to school as their number-one complaint. But unless and until parents and teachers join together as advocates for the common good of youngsters, we will not create serious educational breakthroughs for precisely those children we are most concerned about.[51]

When all the inhabitants of a school—the students, parents, teachers, and administrators—are there because they agree on and believe in the kind of education practiced by that school because they have a shared sense of that particular school's educational mission, what goes on there can be both positive and powerful.

The Search for Diversity

Many parents, both privileged and less than privileged, have discovered that there are approaches to schooling that differ markedly from the traditional elementary, middle, and high schools with which they are familiar. These approaches include Montessori schools, open/integrated-day schools, Waldorf schools, microsociety schools, and schools that specialize in particular aspects of the conventional curriculum, like the fine and performing arts or science and technology. Others break the conventional elementary, middle, high school pattern and run from kindergarten through grade 8, occasionally from preschool through high school. Many of these schools don't stress the simple accumulation of traditional skills and knowledge but rather are aimed at the full intellectual, social, and moral development of children and young people. Inquisitive parents who don't find these possibilities offered in their local public schools often take the only other courses open to them: they put their children in nonpublic schools where such options do exist, or they become active advocates of home schooling, charters, or vouchers. In every case the local school district loses their interest and support.

One basic reason for the lack of true diversity and choice in our local public schools—even in those cases where diversity and choice are thought to be desirable—is the way we attempt to introduce such a radical change. We are well aware of the enormous inertia and resistance to change inherent in any large social institution, be it an automobile company or a school system, but we are hard pressed to figure out ways to overcome that inertia. It does little good simply to tell each existing neighborhood school in a district that it now has the power—and therefore the autonomy—to develop or adopt its very own innovative approach to schooling, because the parents/professionals in these schools are inevitably people who are not there by choice and have widely differing views about what schooling should be.

Instituting Genuine Diversity and Choice: Stage 1

Perhaps a combination of the approaches developed in New York's District 4 and in the Massachusetts communities of Lowell, Fall River, and Worcester comes closest to working. Under this model,[52] the local school board and the central administration create a genuinely *collaborative* planning effort involving everyone in the community. The first step is to set up a *citywide parent/professional/community planning council*. The council is usually made up of at least one parent representative plus an alternate (who have been elected by the parents) and a teacher representative (who has been elected by the teachers) from each school in the system (or in larger districts, from carefully drawn racially and ethnically integrated subdistricts). Interested principals should also be invited to join the group, and there should be at least one delegate chosen by the administrators union. The president of the local teachers union should also be a member, along with several members from the larger community (businesspeople and social workers, for example). Council members have a duty to keep the constituencies they represent informed of what the council is doing. There should also be many reports in the local media, since all council meetings should be open to the public. The council has two main jobs:

1. *Do research on existing systems of diversity and choice.* The council must first gather information on what other cities and school systems have done in the past and may be doing now to create a wide range of educational options—in other words, investigate the different kinds of public schools that have been established and may still be in operation

throughout the country. Ideally, teams of parents, teachers, and principals should visit as many of these schools as possible and see them in operation. This research should be condensed into a detailed list that will prove to parents and educators alike that public schools do not have to be all the same. This is the crucial first step in building the constituency for diversity and choice and thus the constituency against the educational uniformity of authoritarian standards and high-stakes tests.

2. *Prepare and conduct parent/professional surveys.* The council should now take the information it has gathered and convert it into two closely linked surveys (translated into all appropriate languages) related to elementary and middle school options. Whatever options are later developed at the high school level should be continuations of those instituted lower down. The first survey is sent to the parents of all preschool and elementary-age children in the district—including the parents of children attending nonpublic preschools and elementary schools. (However, it may not be easy to gain the latter's cooperation once the private and parochial schools realize that the public schools may be preparing to offer their kind of schooling within the public system.) The second survey is sent to all teachers and principals in the district.

Designing and Administering the Surveys

The surveys should solicit answers to these questions:

- Do the parents *want* to be able to choose the schools their children will attend?
- Do the teachers and principals *want* to be able to choose the kind of schooling they will practice?
- What kinds of schooling do parents wish their local school system to make available?
- Would parents be willing to have their children travel at public expense in order to attend a chosen school?
- Are there teachers and principals in the system who wish to practice the kinds of schooling parents want?
- What kind of schools would teachers themselves like to see created in the system?
- Would teachers be willing to work on planning teams with parents to create the schools both they and parents want?

- Would teachers and principals be willing to transfer voluntarily to a new building in order to practice the kind of schooling they and the parents want?
- Do current administrative and teacher union contracts permit such voluntary transfers without regard to seniority?
- Could contracts be renegotiated to allow such transfers?
- What is the respondent's race/ethnicity?
- Where are the parent's children currently attending school? What grade are they in?
- Where is the teacher currently teaching? At what grade level?

The survey should then solicit opinions regarding between five and ten different types of schools it believes the parents and teachers of its school system would be most interested in. Each type should be distinct, not a minor variation on the traditional school (although the traditional school must be one of the options). Some possible options include:

- Padeaia schools, advocated by Mortimer Adler, in which the curriculum is heavily weighted toward the "great books" and teaching most often takes place in one-on-one coaching sessions and Socratic seminars.
- "Core knowledge" schools, advocated by E. D. Hirsch, Jr., in which students become "culturally literate" in the established disciplines of the Western world, largely through conventional whole-class instruction.
- "Continuous progress" schools, in which students are assigned to classes in the traditional subjects according to achievement levels (in other words, a student may be in an advanced math class but in an average reading class).
- Two way bilingual schools, in which English speakers and students who speak another language (Spanish, for example) are taught together in classes using both English and the other language and all the students become bilingual.
- Montessori schools, in which students operate freely within a "prepared environment" using a wide variety of specially designed manipulative materials.
- Open education or "integrated day" schools, in which classrooms are filled with age-appropriate books and hands-on learning materials and students alternate between individual and group work.

- Waldorf schools, based on the educational ideas of Rudolf Steiner, in which the curriculum is rich with artistic and social activities.
- "Multiple intelligence" schools, based on the developmental ideas put forth by Howard Gardner.
- Microsociety schools, in which students develop and operate their own small democratic society.

A second range of choices should describe the different kinds of curricular specializations that any of the basic types of schools described above could offer as an additional attraction: science and technology, the fine and performing arts, immersion in a foreign language, etc.

Surveys like this "force" a choice, because respondents have a limited number of clearly defined options and must order their preferences. Open-ended what-kind-of-school-would-you-like questionnaires almost always produce a long shopping list of desirable features that may or may not fit together into a coherent educational program and may or may not, when put together by system planners, be what the respondents had in mind.

Experience has shown that sending the parent survey home with the students and asking that it be returned the same way (then forwarding it to the central office for compilation and analysis) produces the highest response rate. This is not a sampling survey but rather an attempt to discover the actual number of parents who want choice and what their choices are. No attempt should be made to generalize beyond the number of respondents and the choices they make.

The parent surveys provide the council, the central administrators, and the local school board with the following types of information:

- An overall indication of the degree to which parents respond positively to choosing the kind of schooling their children should receive.
- A ranking of the educational choices parents have made, from most desired to least desired. This gives a general idea of how many of what kinds of schools would be necessary to satisfy parent demand for each option.
- Whether enough parents in an existing school have chosen a particular option so that the school might possibly be converted into one delivering that kind of education.
- Which options desired by parents are not concentrated in any existing school and would therefore need to be set up as brand-new citywide schools drawing a student body from all over the district.

- The number of parents who would allow their children to be bused at public expense in order to get their first choice of schooling.
- A rough idea of the minority/nonminority balance in schools based on parental choice. (This is crucial information since school choice is one of the primary methods of achieving integration.)

The teacher/principal surveys provide the following information:

- A ranking of the educational choices made by teachers and principals.
- A general idea of how the teacher/principal choices break down in each existing school.
- The number of teachers (and principals) who would be willing to transfer voluntarily from their present schools in order to practice the kind of education they have chosen.

Based on all this information, the council should be able to determine whether a workable match exists between the kinds of schooling parents want for their children and the kinds of schooling teachers and principals wish to practice.

If the surveys indicate that a large segment of both groups want diversity and choice, the council can officially recommend to both the superintendent of schools and the local school board that the district carefully plan and implement a system of educational choices.

Unexpected Survey Results

When Lowell and Worcester conducted their planning processes and administered their surveys back in the 1980s, most observers (including some of us who were helping these school districts identify their choices and prepare and administer the surveys) expected that many parents, especially those who were poor and/or minority, might not be inclined to make such choices (or would not believe they were capable of making such choices). Some people predicted that the return rate would be fairly low, perhaps as low as 10 percent of the city's total public elementary school parent population. We were also warned that if the parents did choose, they would select mostly the old-fashioned, highly academic schools they were accustomed to, and that teachers and principals might be the only ones who would choose the more innovative models.

None of these expectations turned out to be the case. The Worcester parent survey return rates never dropped below 50 percent and at times ran as high as 80 percent. These returns also accurately reflected the minority/nonminority percentages of the system's parent population, thus refuting any expectation that poor and minority parents either would not respond or would not choose the schools they wanted for their children.

Further, the models most requested by parents were *not* good old-fashioned schools concentrating on teaching "the basics." In Lowell, the two most popular models were the fine and performing arts and the microsociety schools (which were then created as new citywide schools). In Worcester, enough parents, both minority and nonminority, selected the Montessori school to guarantee not only that one could open but that it would be perfectly integrated. (This school was not created, because not enough teachers were interested in teaching there.) By substantial margins it was the *parents* in both cities who wanted the more adventurous, innovative models and the teachers and principals who wanted the more traditional schools. Not only that, it was the poor and minority parents, not the white middle-class parents, who more often selected the more progressive models.

Stage 2: Creating Small, Community-Connected Schools

Of course, a diversity of educational philosophies, pedagogical approaches, curricula, and school organizations is impossible to create in the face of state-imposed one-size-fits-all standards and one-size-fits-all standardized testing. The first thing any local district must do is apply for a waiver of these imposed requirements and at the same time submit its own plan for setting up diverse schools and assessing the success or failure of these schools. (See Chapter 8 for a suggested assessment plan.) This request ideally should be backed up by a community referendum stating that the district has the right to make its own educational decisions. If the waiver is denied, the school board and central administration should seriously consider acting independently of the state mandates anyway.

Once the waiver has been granted (or its independence declared), the district has the difficult task of creating the kinds of schools the parents and teachers have asked for. Assuming the schools parents want are roughly the same schools teachers and principals want and are thus able to provide, district administrators should develop a model of what the new system would look like—how many parents and teachers have chosen which schools and thus how many of each kind of school will be needed, which parents and teachers have chosen which option, and what those choices mean in terms of getting students from one place to another.

The Need for Small Schools

A 1999 study conducted by Mary Ann Raywid, of Hofstra University, compared rural, suburban, and inner-city students who attended small schools with their counterparts who attended large schools. Raywid found that "students attending smaller schools have higher graduation rates, better attendance, fewer discipline problems, higher achievement, and greater satisfaction with school. Faculty in small schools, when compared with faculty in large schools with similar groups of students, report much higher morale." These findings, she says, have been "confirmed with a clarity and a level of confidence rare in the annals of education research."[53]

Similarly, a 2001 report issued by the Center for School Change at the University of Minnesota studied twenty-four schools across the nation and concluded that smaller schools (around four hundred students) are both more cost effective and do a better job with students. Student learning improves in these more intimate settings. The report also recommended that smaller schools can and should be combined and share space with other community agencies and services such as libraries, health clinics, recreation centers, colleges, and preschool and senior programs. When students get to know teachers and feel connected to their communities, test scores and graduation rates go up and discipline problems go down, and families, students, and teachers report greater satisfaction with the educational experience.[54]

Learning from this research, local districts planning for diversity and choice should limit school size to no more than four hundred students. Some of these schools can and will be new schools located in new space. Existing school buildings designed to hold larger numbers of students can be divided into a number of smaller four-hundred-student schools, thus giving students options without their having to leave the neighborhood. In New York's District 4 this is the standard approach—large existing schools have been closed and reopened as shared facilities housing up to five small schools.[55]

A Final Cautionary Word

Most districts that have instituted even small amounts of diversity and choice have gone about creating new schools and converting existing neighborhood, nonchoice schools into schools of choice slowly and carefully, giving everyone involved—parents, students, and professional staff—time to get used to the process and recognize its advantages. Moving too fast is one sure way to generate resistance to such a revolutionary change in the way most of our local districts do business.

8

The New Educational Civil Rights Movement

Despite everything I have said here against the standards-and-testing movement, I don't wish to imply that the governors and legislators, the corporate leaders and foundation executives, the state bureaucrats, or even the educational union leaders and college and university professors who support and/or implement the standards-and-testing agenda are evil people, or that they are they all ultraconservative "right wingers." They inhabit every niche of the political spectrum, and they truly believe that what they are advocating is in the best interests of the nation and its schoolchildren—especially those who are poor and/or members of minorities. But a growing number of parents, teachers, front-line school administrators, school board members, and leading educational thinkers now believe that this "school reform" movement is at best misguided, that its proponents must be convinced that their approach will not produce the results they are looking for, and that what they are doing is causing irreparable harm.

The Need and the Prospects for Integration

Just because the past fifty years have not been kind to our aspirations for a high-quality racially, ethnically, and economically integrated system of public education, this does not mean that the next fifty must be a continuation of those less-than-successful efforts. One of the lessons those years has taught us is that—given that we are still a society divided by racially, ethnically, and economically identifiable housing and employment patterns—any attempt at true integration of our public schools is going to be extraordinarily difficult, perhaps even impossible.

We have also learned that while desegregation efforts must involve a degree of constitutional and therefore court-directed coercion, that coercion must be as limited as possible. For many of us, the scenes of white citizens of South Boston resisting "forced busing" in 1974 by hurling stones at buses carrying black children to South Boston High School are still all too vivid. The most peaceful and effective efforts at desegregation, especially in the North, have been the largely voluntary desegregation plans—like those in Buffalo and more recently in Boston—based on magnet schools, educational diversity, and carefully controlled parent choice. If any desegregation plan is going to be successful, it must be based on the rule of few sticks and many carrots. But other factors enter in as well.

First, suburban parents will not volunteer to have their children attend our urban schools as long as Kozol's "savage inequalities" exist between our urban and suburban school districts. These fiscal and educational disparities have to be erased if we are to have any hope of metropolitan desegregation. But metropolitanization in some form is obviously necessary. That is, we need to create—and our courts will have to uphold—the creation of metropolitan districts in which inner-city and contiguous suburban districts are joined for the specific purpose of voluntary, choice-based desegregation. State and the federal governments then need, at a minimum, to fund both urban and suburban interdistrict magnet schools and provide transportation to these schools.

Second, simply creating a system of interdistrict magnet schools is probably not going to overcome the enormous and in many respects legitimate (i.e., nonracist) power of the neighborhood school. After all, it is comforting to be able to have your children walk to a nearby school (even though many parents seem quite happy to put their children on buses to transport them to private schools).

What we need, then, is something we have never had before—the voluntary banding together of all the school districts in a given metropolitan area *and all of that metropolitan area's cultural, artistic, civic, business, and higher-education institutions* in a program that offers all children and young people access to all of those institutions. This is not be simply a desegregation device. Rather, it should be part of the much larger attempt to build a high-quality metropolitan system of public schooling, one rooted in what Richardson, Bruner, Gardner, Howe, Sarason, and other educational thinkers believe to be the proper way to go about educating children and young people—a system in which children and young people, to borrow Richardson's phrasing, are "asked to learn the matters governing the lives of their parents and communities; the laws of motion of the local and national economy; the management of resources, people, and processes within them; local and national political administration; the structure and functions of institutions, and so on" rather than studying "artificial, made-up subjects that are not embedded in cultural practice."

By cultural practice, Richardson means "not just hardware and technological tools, but all of the economic and administrative institutions through which our complex societies operate. Being fully intelligent means having access to, and cognitive grasp of, those cultural tools, and the powers through which they operate."

This approach to school learning would be "tied into meaningful cultural activity" and would attempt to "reconnect the cognitive systems of individual [students] with the cultural systems in which they are immersed through a more active system of cultural involvement. For example, local producers and practitioners can be invited to submit genuine problems to the schools, requiring thought, knowledge, research, and practical solution.

"The news agent may have a delivery organization problem, the parish council a reporting problem, the steelworks a marketing problem, the engineer a component design problem, the health centre a health education problem, the shirt factory another kind of design problem, the farmer all kinds of botanical and zoological problems, and so on.

"Within such cultural activities, all the aims and objectives of any accepted curriculum—the development of skills of literacy and numeracy, literature and scientific research, computer use, local and national history, geography, physics, biology, design, commerce, and so on—could be worked out. But they would be worked out in meaningful contexts that would not only help develop abstract concepts in a grounded way, but also engender economic sense, a sense of activities in schools being worthwhile, as well as civic identity and responsibility. It may also avoid the semienforced digestion of prepackaged, dead skills and knowledge, which turns school into a race of motivation and persistence, and which, in turn, stifles so much intelligence."[56]

The city of Boston planned but never implemented an approach similar to this in the early 1970s as part of its 1975 Bicentennial celebration. The program was called The City As Educator (or CAE) and was designed to serve twenty thousand kindergarten through grade 12 students drawn voluntarily from Boston's then segregated schools. The intention was that it would eventually become a metropolitan desegregation program.[57]

Under this plan equal numbers of white and minority parents could choose an education for their child that took place primarily in a collaborative network encompassing all of Boston's arts and cultural institutions, its science and technology resources, its charitable, civic, and governmental agencies, its businesses and industries, and the area's colleges and universities. This education would take a completely different approach to the use of school staff and school facilities.

The program would be set up by the public school system, the other private and public host institutions, and the city authority responsible for building schools. Institutions proposed/recruited included the Boston Museum of Fine Arts, the Children's Museum, the Institute of Contemporary Art, the Boston Symphony, the Boston Ballet, the Boston Opera Company, the Boston Public Library and its branches, the New England Conservatory of Music, local theater companies, the Franklin Park Zoo, the Massachusetts Horticultural Society, the Museum of Science, the Museum of Transportation, the New England Aquarium, the Animal Rescue League, the Massachusetts Audubon Society, the Arnold Arboretum, Logan Airport, Massachusetts General Hospital, Harvard's Museum of Comparative Zoology and Smithsonian Observatory, Boston's City Hall, the police department and local courts (county, state, and federal), the State House and Legislature, the local gas, electric, and telephone companies, the Boston Bar Association and some larger law firms, the Federal Reserve Bank and major local banks, the John Hancock and Prudential Insurance Companies, the Polaroid and Honeywell Corporations, the Boston Redevelopment Authority, Harvard University, the Massachusetts Institute of Technology, Boston University, and the University of Massachusetts at Boston.

Institutions that owned and operated private or public facilities (and most of them did) would agree either to rent space in those buildings to the school system or to create new jointly designed and jointly used space paid for by city and state funds that would normally go toward building new conventional schools. These "learning resource centers" would be set up *in or next to* each major cooperating institution.

Students in the CAE program would attend classes in their local school on alternate weeks. The other weeks they and their teachers would spend in one of the racially integrated "resource centers." Each center was to be staffed jointly by teachers and host institution staff members. Since during any given week half of each CAE school's student population would be at a resource center, roughly half the normal school space would be needed.

An accompanying new, interdisciplinary, hands-on, developmental curriculum was developed that would allow the students to use the resource centers to explore firsthand "real world" resources not available in a conventional school. During their "in school" weeks students would reflect on this firsthand experience and prepare for their next resource center visit.

Instead of trying to make sense of life and the world by studying *about it* in dreary textbooks and other second- and thirdhand "educational" materials, students would be able to study real animals at the zoo and the Audubon nature preserves; real trees and plants at the Arboretum; real aquatic life at the Aquarium; real art and cultural life in the city's museums, concert halls, and theatres; the real world of the sciences at the Museum of Science and in college and university laboratories; the real world of business and industry in banks, business offices, the Federal Reserve, industrial plants, and retail stores; the real political life of the city, state, and country at City Hall, the State House, and the federal office buildings; the real workings of the justice system in the city's police department and its municipal, state, and federal courts; the real operation (and occasionally nonoperation) of the transportation system at the Transit Authority, Logan Airport, and the city's rail stations. And so on and so on.

We CAE planners did not expect to put such an elaborate system in place in the short space of three or four years; but we did want to have a pilot project up and running in time for the Bicentennial. Unfortunately the Bicentennial and a federal court desegregation order arrived at the same moment. The agonies and disruptions triggered by the desegregation crisis ruined any chance that the city could think or do anything about long-range educational innovations such as the City As Educator program. The plan was abandoned. (We developed a similar plan, called the Career Development Center Network, for the city of Chicago, but it sank in the swamp of Chicago educational politics.)

Nevertheless, such a program could be the basis for an effective interdistrict desegregation plan. Obviously, it would require intensive collaborative planning between the urban and suburban school districts—not to mention convincing suburban parents that the program was educationally irresistible. But the vast array of potentially educational public and private institutions exists only in our inner cities, not in the largely residential suburbs. For suburban children to have the benefits of an education conducted in alliance with those institutions, their parents would need to overcome their prejudices against urban life and agree to have their children brought to those urban resource centers.

The Need and Prospects for Fiscal Equality

The *Rodriguez* language suggesting that the fiscal inequality between school districts should not necessarily be maintained offers some hope of reestablishing the *Brown* assertion that public education and the state provision of such education on equal terms are federal constitutional rights. Doing so would require that one of the state constitutionality suits be appealed to the Supreme Court, that it be accepted by that Court, and that the Court accept Justice Marshall's dissent and overturn the *Rodriguez* decision. Given the current composition of the Rehnquist Court and in light of possible additional appointments by the Bush administration, such a scenario appears most unlikely.

The Need and Prospects for Local Control

The *Rodriguez* decision does, however, offer some hope of restoring the great American tradition of local district and therefore local citizen control of the content and procedures of elementary and secondary education. As the majority opinion in that case put it back in 1973:

> In an era that has witnessed a consistent trend toward centralization of the functions of government, local sharing of responsibility for public education has survived. The merit of local control was recognized in both the majority and dissenting opinions in *Wright v Council of the City of Emporia*. Mr. Justice Stewart stated there that "direct control over decisions vitally affecting the education of one's children is a need that is strongly felt in our society." The Chief Justice in his dissent agreed that local control is not only vital to continued public support of the schools, but it is of overriding importance from an educational standpoint as well.
>
> The persistence of attachment to government at its lowest level where education is concerned reflects the depth of commitment of its supporters. In part local control means . . . the freedom to devote more money to the education of one's children. Equally important, however, is the opportunity it offers for participation in the decision-making process that determines how those local dollars will be spent. Each locality is free to tailor local programs to local needs. Pluralism also affords some opportunity for experimentation, innovation, and a healthy competition for educational excellence. An analogy to the Nation-State relationship in our federal system seems uniquely appropriate. Mr. Justice Brandeis identified as one of the peculiar strengths of our form of government each state's freedom to "serve as a laboratory; to try novel social and economic experiments." No area of social concern stands to profit more from a multiplicity of viewpoints and from a diversity of approaches than does public education.

Further, Justice William Brennan found in his dissent, "Here, there can be no doubt that education is inextricably linked to the right to participate in the electoral process and to the rights of free speech and association guaranteed by the First Amendment."[58]

A federal court case based on both the Fourteenth and First Amendments could reinstate local control of the content and procedures of elementary and secondary education, including the rights of both parents and local educators to make the fundamental decisions concerning the intellectual content and educational pedagogy practiced in their local schools. This is a legal strategy well worth pursuing.

Also Needed: A Diversity of Standards and Assessments

Being against the imposition of any single set of solely academic standards and any single high-stakes, solely academic test (which together add up to establishing a single, solely academic intellectual orthodoxy) is not to say that there can or should be no high educational expectations and no system of public accountability in American public schooling. *But before any fair, equal, and just system of accountability can be designed and certainly before any such system can be implemented, the three flagrant violations of the human rights of students, parents, and professional educators listed earlier must be addressed and remedied.*

There can be no fairness, no equality, and no justice in any assessment system until and unless a truly level playing field has been established, until and unless Kozol's savage inequalities are remedied. There can be no "equality of educational opportunity" until and unless our underfunded inner-city and rural schools and districts are brought up to minimum suburban funding standards, until and unless ancient, crumbling buildings are repaired, until and unless classes of between thirty-five and forty-five students are reduced to twenty, until and unless undertrained and underpaid teachers are replaced with well-trained, well-paid teachers, until and unless ancient educational materials and electronic equipment are replaced, and until and unless adequate support services, including early childhood education for every child who is poor and/or a member of a minority, are provided to help children and young people and their families who are living lives of quiet desperation and extreme poverty in their communities outside school.

A Proposed Assessment System

Assuming that a truly level playing field has been created, any fair, just, and equal system of assessment would have to be divided into two equal parts.

The first part would assess *the amount and quality of the resources* children and young people are receiving in the schools they attend, beginning with whether every school in every local school district really does meet the level-playing-field criteria but moving on to whether each school meets the *Claremont* criteria. That is, in addition to the more easily determined measures of fiscal, facilities, and curricular equity, believable measures would need to be developed and used to determine whether a school meets acceptable levels of equality with regard to relationships, race, culture and class, values, teaching and learning, safety, physical environment, hope, and the process of change.

The second part of the assessment would deal in greater detail with the teaching and learning process, specifically with two vital questions. First, is the local school district and the particular school a student attends providing that student with an education aimed at "the full development" of her or his personality—that is, is the development of *all* of *every* student's intellectual, social, artistic, and moral capacities the foundation of the school's stated operational mission? Second, is the school successfully providing students with Sarason's "contexts of productive learning" and Richardson's "socially meaningful context for learning"—that is, does it genuinely assist *all* of its students to develop all of their intellectual, social, artistic, and moral capacities?

Designing a Fair, Just, and Equal Assessment System

In order to arrive at ways to assess this broad range of school and student achievements, the parents and professional staff of each public school established by choice must spell out in considerable detail what that school conceives its specific educational mission to be, including the ways the school proposes to reach these goals. What are the school's intellectual (rather than "academic") standards? What and how should teachers teach and students learn? What and how will the school measure to find out if it is providing the education it intends to?

If a school decides that a standardized test would be useful, it is free to use one, making sure that the test:

- Covers only what students have been taught.
- Is based on standards developed by teachers.
- Is not used as the sole basis for high-stakes decisions.
- Minimizes disruption to students' learning.
- Provides useful and timely diagnostic information to teachers.
- Recognizes that meaningful school change occurs over many years.
- Acknowledges that not everything that is taught can be tested.
- Complements rather than drives teaching and learning.

Test results should also be released to the public each time the test is administered.[59]

Assessment and accountability planning like this might look something like the "authentic" system advocated by the Coalition for Authentic Reform in Education (CARE), a Massachusetts group of parent-teacher-citizen activists opposed to the Massachusetts Comprehensive Assessment System (MCAS). CARE's proposed system (with my additions and emendations in brackets) consists of:

- *Local assessments* using an assessment and accountability plan developed by the parents and staff of each school based on a short list of basic competencies and on each school's goals. The plan should explain how the school will assess students (including the use of portfolios and many other criteria), how decisions such as graduation and promotion will be made, and how assessment information will be reported to parents, students, teachers, the community, and the state. Graduation will be decided by the local school district, not the state.

- *Limited standardized testing* in literary and numeracy only, with all such tests not used to make high-stakes decisions about students but only as one additional source of information about both students and their schools. [Parents opposed to such testing should have the basic human right to have their children opt out of these tests, just as teachers and other school officials opposed to such testing should have the professional right not to administer the tests. One of the two national teacher unions, the National Education Association, has now officially endorsed this parental right.]

- *Annual school reporting* on progress or lack of progress toward stated goals and very minimal state standards. The report will be based on local assessments broken down by race and ethnicity, gender, socioeconomic status, special needs, and limited English proficiency and will include the results of any standardized tests used. [The report should also indicate how many parents (if any) have taken their children out of the school and why, how many teachers (if any) have left the school and why, how many children are on the waiting list if the school is oversubscribed, and how many teachers are waiting to join the staff and why.] The report is reviewed by each school's local school council, parents and community members, the district, and the state. When necessary, the state or district may send in teams to verify the accuracy of a school's report.

- *School Quality Reviews (SQRs)*. Every four to five years, a team of experts chosen by the state department of education or the regional accreditation association visits the school for three days, interviewing students, educators, and parents; sitting in on classes; looking at examples of student work; and so on. The team then presents a detailed report to help guide the school in its annual planning and reporting.[60]

A rigorous, locally determined assessment system such as this must be submitted to state education authorities to support a request for a waiver from state-mandated curricula and tests.

The Ultimate Assessment Provided by Choice

The principle of limited "free market" public education for both parents and teachers is a way not only for individual schools to improve their quality but also a way for the overall quality of the system to improve. Any school losing a large number of students and teachers is clearly a school in trouble and a candidate for intense scrutiny by the local school authorities and possibly for closure and "reconstitution." A school for which there is a waiting list is clearly a successful school.

The Responsibilities of Diversity and Choice

The fair, just, and equal American educational system advocated here clearly requires a new set of responsibilities at each level of the educational/political hierarchy. For instance, after a school has "spelled out in considerable detail what that school conceives its educational mission to be," the locally elected school board and its central administration, acting as the agents of state government, must review and approve the school's mission and goals to make sure they fall within the broad limits of democratic belief and practice and the U.S. Constitution and then monitor the school's performance *as measured against that school's stated goals* each year. The local school board (with state and federal assistance) also needs to provide fair and equal funding for its schools and oversee their fiscal and administrative management. The state would need to monitor the civil rights performance of local school districts and make sure every school in every district is equally and adequately funded. And the federal government would need to monitor the civil rights performance of the states and make sure that the schools of every state are equally and adequately funded. *No savage inequalities can be permitted anywhere.*

Not a New Idea

The educational system being proposed here is hardly a new idea. In the latter part of the nineteenth century, Alfred Russel Wallace, the co-constructor with Charles Darwin of the theory of evolution by natural selection, set forth these same ideas:

> In our present society the bulk of the people have no opportunity for the full development of all their powers and capacities. . . . The accumulation

of wealth is now mainly effected by the misdirected energy of competing individuals; and the power that wealth so obtained gives them is often used for purposes which are hurtful to the nation. There can be no true individualism, no fair competition, without equality of opportunity for all. This alone is social justice, and by this alone can the best that is in each nation be developed and utilised for the benefit of all its citizens. . . .

Equality of opportunity is absolute fair play as between man and man [Wallace's definition of "man" would very much include women, since he was a strong advocate of women's suffrage and all women's rights] in the struggle for existence. It means that all shall have the best education they are capable of receiving; that their faculties shall all be well trained, and their whole nature obtain the fullest moral, intellectual, and physical development. This does not mean that we shall all have the same education, that all shall be made to learn the same things and go through the same training, but that all shall be so trained as to develop fully all that is best in them. It must be an adaptive education, modified in accordance with the peculiar mental and physical nature of the pupils, not a rigid routine applied to all alike, as is too often the case now.[61]

9

What Can and Must Be Done: A Proposed Action Agenda

Federal courts in Florida, Texas, and Louisiana have ruled that those states have the right to set academic standards and administer a single test to all students to determine whether those standards are being met, even though poor and minority students in those states are failing the tests at an alarming rate. This suggests that until these decisions are set aside by the Supreme Court, all states are free to pursue their present autocratic, undemocratic course. Concerned parents, teachers, school administrators, and test experts are therefore preparing to take their challenge of the standards-and-testing agenda all the way to the top.

But legal action is not our only recourse. As in the last century's civil rights movement, every segment of American society needs to be mobilized to protest the standards-and-testing outrages. Actions like test boycotts and other forms of civil disobedience taken by parents, teachers, school administrators, and school boards take on paramount importance.

It is all well and good for someone like me, too ancient or decrepit to serve any longer in the front lines, to urge parents and professionals still in the trenches to rebel and suffer the consequences. But if they also serve who only sit and write, here is a brief educational civil rights action agenda.

Legal Action

1. Urge organizations like FairTest, the American Civil Liberties Union, the National Association for the Advancement of Colored People, People for the American Way, and minority groups of all stripes to bring more suits against the state and federal government protesting the disparate and unequal effects a single standardized curriculum and

74

a single standardized high-stakes test have on poor, minority, special-needs, and vocational students.

2. Urge urban and rural school districts to continue to file state (and eventually federal) lawsuits arguing for fiscal equality.

3. Raise the legal/IRS question of "nonprofit" "nonpolitical" foundations that support unequal educational opportunities. Foundations are not supposed to "lobby" for political ends.

4. Raise legal and legislative questions about exempting private and parochial schools from curricular standards and high-stakes testing. State boards of education are responsible for *all* schools, nonpublic as well as public. (Goring the nonpublic-school ox with the standards-and-testing bull may be the best way to kill the whole movement.)

5. Expose corporation and right-wing foundation support for organizations such as Achieve and the National Center for Education and the Economy.

Action in Higher Education

1. Organize schools of education and individual faculty members to protest the standards-and-testing agenda as an abridgment of academic freedom.

2. Organize similar protests by arts and science faculties.

Action by Professional Associations/Unions

1. Urge all K–12 superintendent, principal, and teacher organizations to explore the possibility of taking First Amendment "academic freedom" legal action.

2. Urge national, state, and local associations/unions, especially the teacher unions, to take strong policy positions opposing curricular and assessment control by the state and federal government and stressing parental and professional (and elected local school board) control.

Action by Citizen Groups

1. Urge state and local school boards, PTAs, PTOs, and the like to issue strong policy statements opposing the standards-and-testing agenda.

2. Support independent parent/citizen groups like Massachusetts Citizens for the Public Schools.

3. Organize local, state, and national parent (and student if backed by parents) test boycotts.
4. Organize boycotts of corporations and businesses that support the standards-and-testing agenda.
5. Instigate the community planning process described in Chapter 7.

Action by Individuals

1. Join protest groups such as CARE and PURE.
2. Support student and parent test boycotts.
3. Boycott businesses and corporations that support the standards-and-testing movement.
4. Donate money to organizations such as FairTest.

Is There Hope?

It's up to us. It will take a new educational civil rights movement such as the one proposed here to bring about the kind of just, fair, equal, and thus truly democratic system of American public education we deserve. Otherwise, we are in for yet another century of educational injustice. We must not let that happen.

Sources of Information and Assistance

The National Center for Fair and Open Testing (FairTest)
342 Broadway
Cambridge, MA
02139
(617) 864-4810
FAX (617) 497-2224
info@fairtest.org

The Coalition for Authentic Reform in Education (CARE)
c/o FairTest as above
www.fairtest.org/care

The Center for Collaborative Education
1573 Madison Avenue
Room 201
New York, NY
10029
(212) 348-7821

The National Center for Restructuring Education,
        Schools and Teaching
Teachers College
Columbia University
New York, NY
10027
(212) 678-3432

Center for Public School Renewal (CPSR)
372 Middleton Drive
Ann Arbor, MI
48105
(734) 747-9421
educate2@mediaone.net

Institute for Responsive Education
21 Lake Hall

Northeastern University
Boston, MA
02115
(617) 373-5813
ire@neu.edu

Cross City Campaign for Urban School Reform
407 South Dearborn Street
Suite 1725
Chicago, IL
60605
(312) 322-4880

Notes

Chapter 1

1. *Brown v Board of Education of Topeka,* Kay, et al, Appeal from the United States District Court for the District of Kansas, Supreme Court of the United States, 347 U.S. 483, decided May 17, 1954.

2. Gary Orfield and John T. Yen, "Resegregation in American Schools," Harvard Civil Rights Project (June, 1999), p. 3.

3. Ibid, p. 34.

4. Ibid, p. 22.

5. *Milliken v Bradley,* U.S. Supreme Court, 418 U.S. 717 (1974).

6. *San Antonio Independent School District v Rodriguez,* U.S. Supreme Court, 411 U.S. I (1973).

7. Jonathan Kozol and Paul Wellstone, *The New York Times,* March 13, 2001, p. A25.

8. *The Boston Globe,* May 31, p. A4.

9. Universal Declaration of Human Rights, 1998 edition, United Nations Department of Public Information, Office of the United Nations High Commissioner for Human Rights, Geneva, Switzerland.

Chapter 2

10. *Milliken v Bradley,* p. 35.

11. *San Antonio,* p. 39.

12. *Educational Equity in Vermont* (Montpelier, VT: Vermont State Department of Education, 1998).

13. Bob Peterson, Kathy Swope, and Barbara Miner, *The Return of Separate and Unequal* (Milwaukee, WI: Rethinking Schools, 2001).

14. Docket No. 312236, Superior Court, San Francisco, CA.

15. *San Antonio, Independent School District v Rodriguez,* U.S. Supreme Court 411 U.S. I (1973), p. 20.

Chapter 3

16. *Boston Globe,* May 20, 2001, p. A42.

17. Ibid.

18. D. E. Miller, "Problems with Studying Vouchers," *Chronicle of Higher Education,* July 13, 2001, p. 23.

Chapter 4

19. Gary Miron and Brooks Applegate, *An Evaluation of Student Achievement in Edison Schools Opened in 1995 and 1996* (Kalamazoo: The Evaluation Center, Western Michigan University, 2001).

20. Minutes of the San Francisco, CA, Board of Education, February 13, 2001.

21. Edward Wyatt, "Defeat Aside, Edison Plans to Expand," *The New York Times,* April 1, 2001, p. 25, national edition.

22. Richard Rothstein, "Education and Job Growth," *The New York Times,* May 10, 2000, p. A23.

23. Robert B. Reich, *The Future of Success* (New York: Alfred A. Knopf, 2000), p. 211.

Chapter 5

24. Miron and Applegate.

25. Gerald Bracey, personal communication.

26. *The Massachusetts Comprehensive Assessment System (MCAS) Spring 2001 Standards and Test Items* (Malden, MA: Massachusetts Department of Education, 2001).

27. Robert J. Marzano and John S. Kendall, *Awash in a Sea of Standards* (Aurora, CO: Mid-continent Research for Education and Learning, 1996).

28. See *FairTest Criticizes Decision in TAAS Case* and other newsletters and publications of the National Center for Fair and Open Testing (FairTest), 342 Broadway, Cambridge, MA, 02139, *info@fairtest.org.*

29. *MCAS.*

30. Bill Delaney, "Critics Fear State Test Taking Will Takei Its Toll," *CNN.com,* May 25, 2001.

31. Craig Bolon, "Problems of Test-Based School Ratings," *New Democracy Newsletter,* Boston, MA, February 21, 2001.

32. Press release for *Raising Standards or Raising Barriers?,* edited by Gary Orfield and Mindy L. Kornhaber (New York: Century Foundation Press, 2001).

33. Judith Baker, personal communication.

34. Gary Orfield and Johanna Wald, "High-Stakes Testing Mania Hurts Poor and Minority Students the Most," *The Nation*, May 31, 2001, p. 1.

35. John Mudd, *Dropout Rate Analysis: Boston Public Schools, 1999* (Boston: Massachusetts Advocacy Center, 2000).

36. Harold Howe, "High Stakes Trouble," *American School Board Journal*, May, 2000, p. 59.

37. *The New York Times*, April 13, 2001, pp. 1 and 14.

38. *The New York Times*, May 23, 2001, p. 1.

Chapter 6

39. Thomas Jefferson, "Notes on Virginia and Other Writings," in *Three Thousand Years of Educational Wisdom*, edited by Robert Ulich, pp. 463–64 (Boston: Harvard University Press, 1954).

40. This section is largely culled from Ken Richardson's *The Making of Intelligence*, pp. 204–7 (London: Weidenfield and Nicolson, 1999).

41. Reich, Robert, "Standards for What?," Commentary, *Education Week*, June 20, 2001, pp. 48 and 64.

42. Jacques Sternberg, "For Gatekeepers at Colleges, A Daunting Task of Sorting," *The New York Times*, Sunday, February 27, 2000, pp. A1 and A24.

43. Richard C. Atkinson, "UC Takes a Look at SAT I's Worth," *Sacramento Bee*, February 21, 2001, editorial page.

44. See Mary Poplin and Joseph Weeres, *Voices from the Inside* (Claremont, CA: The Institute for Education in Transformation, 1992).

45. Howard Gardner, *Developmental Psychology* (Boston: Little Brown, 1982), p. 452.

46. Mihaly Csikszentmihalyi, Kevin Rathunde, and Samuel Whalen, *Talented Teenagers: The Roots of Success and Failure* (New York: Cambridge University Press, 1993), p. 195.

47. Howard Gardner, quoted by Daniel Goleman in *The New York Times Education Life*, November 9, 1986, p. 24.

Chapter 7

48. Susan Ohanian, *One Size Fits Few: The Folly of Educational Standards* (Portsmouth, NH: Heinemann, 1999).

49. Seymour Fliegel and James MacGuire, *Miracle in East Harlem: The Fight for Choice in Public Education* (New York: Random House, 1993).

50. Deborah Meier, personal communication.

51. Ibid.

52. For a more detailed description, see Timothy W. Young and Evans Clinchy, *Choice in Public Education* (New York: Teachers College Press, 1992), pp. 62–68.

53. Mary Anne Raywid, "Current Literature on Small Schools," January, 1999 (Charleston, WV: ERIC Clearinghouse on Small and Rural Schools).

54. Report on School Size, Center for School Change, Humphrey Center, University of Minnesota, Minneapolis, September 12, 2001.

55. Evans Clinchy, ed., *Creating New Schools: How Small Schools Are Changing American Education* (New York: Teachers College Press, 2000).

Chapter 8

56. Richardson 1999.

57. Evans Clinchy and Peter Capernaros, et al., *The City As Educator: A Role for Education in the Bicentennial Program of the City of Boston* (Boston, MA: Educational Planning Associates, Inc., Boston Redevelopment Authority, 1972).

58. *Rodriguez*, p. 35.

59. Policy proposed by the California Teachers Association, June 3, 2001.

60. Policy Statement by the Coalition for Authentic School Reform, National Center for Fair and Open Testing [FairTest], Cambridge, MA.

61. Harry Clements, *Alfred Russel Wallace, Biologist and Social Reformer* (London: Hutchinson, 1983), pp. 96–98.

Bibliography

Berliner, David C., and Bruce J. Biddle. 1995. *The Manufactured Crisis: Myths, Fraud, and the Attack on America's Public Schools.* Reading, MA: Addison-Wesley.

Bracey, Gerald. 1997. *Setting the Record Straight: Responses to Misconceptions About Public Education in the United States.* Alexandria, VA: Association for Supervision and Curriculum Development.

————. 1998. *Put to the Test: An Educator's and Consumer's Guide to Standardized Testing.* Bloomington, IN: Phi Delta Kappa.

————. 2001. *The War Against America's Public Schools: Privatizing Schools, Commercializing Education.* Boston: Allyn and Bacon.

Clinchy, Evans, ed. 1997. *Transforming Public Education: A New Course for America's Future.* New York: Teachers College Press.

————. 1999. *Reforming American Education from the Bottom to the Top.* Portsmouth, NH: Heinemann.

————. 2000. *Creating New Schools: How Small Schools Are Changing American Education.* New York: Teachers College Press.

Duckworth, Eleanor. 1994. *"The Having of Wonderful Ideas" and Other Essays on Teaching and Learning.* New York: Teachers College Press.

Fliegel, Seymour, and James MacGuire. 1993. *Miracle in East Harlem: The Fight for Choice in Public Education.* New York: Random House.

Gould, Stephen Jay. 1981. *The Mismeasure of Man.* New York: Norton.

Howe, Harold II. 1993. *Thinking About Our Kids: An Agenda for American Education.* New York: Free Press.

Heubert, Jay P., and Robert M. Hauser, eds. 1999. *High Stakes: Testing for Tracking, Promotion, and Graduation.* Washington, DC: National Academy Press.

Kohn, Alfie. 1993. *Punished by Rewards: The Trouble with Gold Stars, Incentive Plans, A's, Praise, and Other Bribes.* Boston: Houghton Mifflin.

————. 1999. *The Schools Our Children Deserve: Moving Beyond Traditional Classrooms and "Tougher Standards."* Boston: Houghton Mifflin.

————. 2000. *The Case Against Standardized Testing: Raising Scores, Ruining Schools.* Portsmouth, NH: Heinemann.

McNeil, Linda M. 2000. *Contradictions of School Reform: Educational Costs of Standardized Testing.* New York: Routledge.

Meier, Deborah. 1995. *The Power of Their Ideas: Lessons for America from a Small School in Harlem.* Boston: Beacon.

————. 2002. *In Schools We Trust: Creating Communities of Learning in an Era of Testing and Standardization.* Boston: Beacon.

Meier, Deborah, et al. 2000. *Will Standards Save Public Education?* Boston: Beacon.

Ohanian, Susan. 1999. *One Size Fits Few: The Folly of Educational Standards.* Portsmouth, NH: Heinemann.

————. 2001. *Caught in the Middle: Nonstandard Kids and a Killing Curriculum.* Portsmouth, NH: Heinemann.

Popham, W. James. 2000. *Testing! Testing! What Every Parent Should Know About School Tests.* Boston: Allyn and Bacon.

Richardson, Ken. 1998. *The Origins of Human Intelligence: Evolution, Development, and Psychology.* New York: Routledge.

————. 1999. *The Making of Intelligence.* London: Weidenfeld and Nicholson.

Rothstein, Richard. 1998. *The Way We Were? The Myths and Realities of America's Student Achievement.* New York: The Century Foundation.

Sacks, Peter. 1999. *Standardized Minds: The High Price of America's Testing Culture and What We Can Do to Change It.* Cambridge, MA: Perseus.

Sarason, Seymour. 1982. *The Culture of the School and the Problem of Change.* Boston: Allyn and Bacon.

————. 1993. *The Predictable Failure of Educational Reform: Can We Change Course Before It's Too Late?* San Francisco: Jossey-Bass.

————. 1996. *Revisiting "The Culture of the School and the Problem of Change."* New York: Teachers College Press.

Swope, Kathy, and Barbara Miner, eds. 2000. *Failing Our Kids: Why the Testing Craze Won't Fix Our Schools.* Milwaukee, WI: Rethinking Schools.

Index